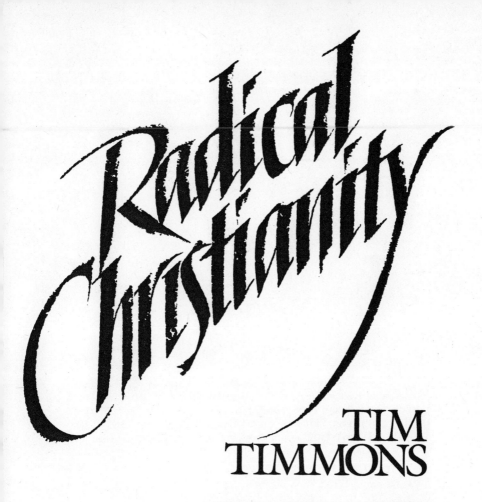

TIM
TIMMONS

Though intended for personal reading
and profit, this book is part of the
Victor Adult Elective Series and
therefore is also intended for group
study. A Leader's Guide with Victor
Multiuse Transparency Masters is
available from your local bookstore.

VICTOR BOOKS

A DIVISION OF SCRIPTURE PRESS PUBLICATIONS INC.
USA CANADA ENGLAND

Most Scripture taken from the *New American Standard Bible,* © the
Lockman Foundation 1960, 1962, 1963, 1968, 1971, 1973, 1975, 1977.
Used by permission. Other quotations are from *The Living Bible* (TLB),
© 1971 by Tyndale House Publishers, Wheaton, IL 60189, and are also
used by permission.

Recommended Dewey Decimal Classification: 248.42
Suggested Subject Heading: CHRISTIAN LIFE AND CONDUCT

Library of Congress Catalog Card Number: 85-63316
ISBN: 0-89693-531-0

© 1986 by Tim Timmons

CONTENTS

Introduction: **On Becoming a Radical 7**

 1 **Radical Christianity 9**
 2 **The Skin of a Reason Stuffed with a Lie 21**
 3 **The Clean Slate Club 33**
 4 **I Got My Act Together but Forgot Where I Put It 43**
 5 **Living on a High Salary 54**
 6 **Supernatural Christianity Naturally 60**
 7 **Normal Christian Living 68**
 8 **A Shot of Spiritual Adrenaline 73**
 9 **When God Becomes *a* God 84**
10 **The Heaven-to-Earth Connection 97**
11 **The Church: A Movement, Not a Monument 108**
12 **How Radical Is Radical? 122**

Appendix: **Living the Radical Christian Life 133**

INTRODUCTION
ON BECOMING
A RADICAL

Radical Christianity is true Christianity.
It works.
Radical Christianity is the only kind of Christianity worth
living.
It transforms lives.
Radical Christianity is living in the power of God.
It is God's plan for changing me, you, and our world.
Radical Christianity is at the core of the Apostle Paul's
letter to the Romans. Paul was a man of strategy, as were
many who helped launch the New Testament church. They
didn't have a lot of time, resources, or help, but they did have
the power of God, and that enabled them to establish new
churches throughout the known world in just a few decades.

Rome was the heart of the civilized world and the capital
of the Roman Empire, a strategic place for establishing and
developing a church whose missionary arms would reach
around the world. Paul gave the Roman church a central place
in his plan to change the world for Christ. The Book of
Romans outlines for the Roman Christians his plan to transform lives through radical Christian living.

Fritz Ridenour wrote a book about Romans entitled

How to Be a Christian Without Being Religious. What a poignant title—and perfectly descriptive of this cornerstone book of the New Testament! We need to know how to be Christians without acting weird, smelling funny, turning people off, or being obnoxiously "spiritual."

Romans tells us how—by being human and radically Christ-centered. It is the key to successful living. Some people call it basic Christianity. Others call it authentic Christianity. I choose to call it *radical* Christianity.

Radical Christianity means getting to the root of things, to the source. It means stripping away the superfluous all the way down to the bottom line, the bare essentials. It means radical change—for us, and for the whole world.

ONE
RADICAL
CHRISTIANITY

*T*wo couples went together to New York City for a vacation. They had reservations at a brand new, beautiful, twenty-nine-story hotel overlooking Central Park. When they arrived at the hotel, they registered, got their keys, and headed upstairs on the elevator. On the way up the bellman told them about the fabulous suite they would be sharing. It featured a bird's-eye view of the park, king-size beds, sunken tubs, and even phones in both bathrooms. After admiring their rooms and unpacking, the vacationers dressed and went out to dinner.

When the two couples returned to the hotel, they were told the elevator wasn't working. They would have to use the stairs—all twenty-nine flights of them! They didn't mind, though; it would give them a chance to work off dinner.

So up the stairs they went. They climbed and they climbed and they climbed, and as they climbed they kept telling themselves how nice those king-size beds were going to feel. As they continued to climb, one of them said, "Why don't we have room service bring us up some dessert when we get there?" They climbed and climbed some more until someone else said, "You know, this is like going to heaven. When we get there we can finally rest." And they kept climbing.

Finally they got to their rooms. One of the guys reached into his pocket for the key. "Hey," he said, "I don't have my key! Do you have yours?" After fumbling in his pocket for a minute, the other guy said, "No, I thought *you* had the key!"

Life is a lot like that. We climb and climb and climb, and as we're climbing we think of all the great things waiting for us. But we arrive at the top without the key. As one executive put it, "I've been climbing my social, corporate, and economic ladder, only to get to the top and find out it was leaning against the wrong building." I'm convinced that's one of the greatest problems people have: They're climbing like crazy, but because their ladders are leaning against the wrong buildings, there's no satisfaction when they get to the top. They haven't got the key.

The Book of Romans gives us the key. It also places the ladder of life against the right building so we're climbing in the right direction. The Apostle Paul says in Romans that Christianity is not just another climb, another religion in which you work your way to God. It's a lifestyle, a radical lifestyle. As my kids say, "It's 'rad,' Dad," which is "valley" talk for, "It's radical." No matter what some people do to it, no matter how they twist and turn it into all kinds of weird and wild things, real Christianity is not just another religion— it's a radical lifestyle.

I'm constantly running into people who tell me, "I tried this brand and this flavor of Christianity, and it really turned my stomach." I agree with them. I've felt a little ill after trying a few of them myself. That's sad, because Christianity is not just another religion—it's rad!

ROMANS: AN OVERVIEW

Paul wrote the Book of Romans before he had visited Rome, but he knew the Romans were an orderly people. That's probably why he divided his letter into several sections. In 1:1-17 he gives us an introduction. Then starting in 1:18 through 3:20 he says in effect that everyone is in a heap of trouble—and no one has an acceptable excuse. I call that section man's predicament.

The next section, 3:21 through chapter 8, deals with God's power. It's divided into three parts: a new past, a new position, and a new power. In the new past (3:21–5:21) Paul explains that when you come into a relationship with God your slate is wiped clean; your past is blotted out. You're justified—just as if you've never sinned, just as if you've never turned away from God. The new position is described in chapter 6. When you are united with Christ in His death and then in His life, a spiritual operation takes place in your heart. You become a new person, you occupy a new position with God, and you are indwelt by the Holy Spirit.

There is a lot of confusion concerning that part, but it clears up in chapters 7 and 8, which deal with the new power. In chapter 7 Paul shares a struggle we all identify with; summarized, it might be, "What I wanted to do, I didn't do, and what I didn't want to do, I did." He's talking to those of us with a pulse! Then in chapter 8 he gives us hope. There is a new power, God Himself, who lives inside you, Paul says— and He frees you from the chains of poor choices. Not that you won't ever make a poor choice again, but you will have the power to consciously make a good one.

Chapters 9 through 11 are an interlude, standing somewhat apart from the rest of the book. I call these three chapters God's preeminence, and they deal with the nation of Israel and the Jewish people. Chapter 9 tells us about the Jewish people in the past and what has happened to them since God first called them—beginning with Abraham. Chapter 10 describes their situation in the present, what's going on with them in the world today. Their future is dealt with in chapter 11. Even though it's set apart from the rest of Romans, it's an exciting interlude.

From man's predicament and God's power and preeminence, we come to man's presentation in chapters 12 through 16. God wants us to present ourselves to Him, "to present your bodies," as Paul says in Romans 12:1.

One year on a vacation our family was going through some of these verses in the car. I was trying to make the point that God wants a *living* sacrifice, so I said, "Back in the Old Testament, God wanted dead animals for sacrifices."

"Yeah, that's right," my kids said in unison. "He wanted dead doves and goats and lambs and stuff."

"Yeah," I said. "But now what God wants in the New Testament, since the Messiah has come, is for *you* to get on the altar."

Tammy, my oldest, sat rather pensively for a few minutes, then said, "Does that mean He wants us to die there?"

"No," I said. "What does it say? He wants us on the altar all right, but He wants us alive." He doesn't want a dead beast, He wants a live human body. That's what Christianity is all about. It's alive. It's radical.

The practical aspect of the previous chapters is picked up in 12 through 14. It's wonderful that you were in real trouble and God got you out of it, that through His power He has saved you from your predicament; but how does that fit in with the real world? Can this Christianity stuff work without giving you a case of the weirds? Paul answers that question head-on by discussing our behavior in relationship to believers—the body of Christ; the government—those in authority over us; and the weak—those who aren't as strong or mature as we are. It's some pretty slippery stuff, but Paul tackles it and tells us how to be Christians in the world without being weird.

There is a conclusion in chapter 15, and in chapter 16 Paul talks about people. He greets twenty-six of them, some "upper crust" and some "common," and each is greeted by name and encouraged.

That tells us something about the early church. As mentioned before, Paul hadn't been to Rome when he wrote this epistle—yet he says hello to twenty-six people who were part of the church there. That means those Roman Christians must have been very mobile, on the move for God. That's just one more aspect of what living a radical Christian lifestyle meant to them.

GETTING RADICAL

I'll say it again: *Christianity is not another religion. It's a radical lifestyle, and a radical lifestyle requires living in the power of God.* Note, for starters, the radical way Paul identifies himself: "Paul, a bond-servant of Christ Jesus, called an apostle, set apart for the Gospel of God" (Rom. 1:1). The same Paul who had become infamous for preaching about freedom in Christ is now calling himself a slave! He calls himself a bond servant, but a bond servant limited only by God. When you're free, truly free, you are only limited by God. When you're not free, you're limited by yourself, other people, or your circumstances. Paul says he's totally free—a slave of Jesus Christ.

The apostle continues with a lengthy greeting until he gets to the verses which are the theme of the book and a preface to everything that follows: "For I am not ashamed of the Gospel, for it is the power of God for salvation to everyone who believes, to the Jew first and also to the Greek. For in it the righteousness of God is revealed from faith to faith; as it is written, 'But the righteous man shall live by faith'" (1:16-17).

From these key verses we can answer questions about the reason for, the result of, and the requirement for a radical lifestyle. Let's look at these one by one.

THE REASON FOR A RADICAL LIFESTYLE

The radical Christian lifestyle has good news—the Gospel. The word *gospel*, like the phrase *born again*, has been distorted and twisted to mean all kinds of things, but literally translated it means simply "good news," news that is welcome and beneficial and needed. "For in it [the Good News] the righteousness of God is revealed from faith to faith" (1:17, brackets added). The word *revealed* means "broken through." In the Good News, the righteousness of God—His rightness, His character—breaks through.

I hesitate to use the following illustration about breaking through, but it's such a great one I'm going to anyway. John Madden, the big guy who used to coach the Oakland Raiders, did a TV commercial for a certain beverage. In it he talked and talked about the qualities of the beverage, referring to a large chart. At the end of the commercial he surprised the viewer—at least the first time—by breaking through the chart. That's the word *revealed*—breaking through. Thus God reveals Himself through the Gospel.

Prior to that, in verse 16, Paul says he is not ashamed of the Gospel; he's not embarrassed by the Good News. Why should he be? It's true! If it weren't true, and he was conning people into believing it, then he would have reason to blush. Some Christians, however, *do* have reason to blush. They act as if the Gospel weren't true and turn Christianity into a con game, burying the Good News with gimmicks and trappings and empty chatter. That's *bad* news!

I constantly encounter people who are searching to see if the Good News is really true. My job is not to force, finagle, or con them into a relationship with God. My job is to search with them, talk with them, answer their questions, and help them discover the truth for themselves. There's no need to con or coerce people into accepting Christianity, and there's nothing to be embarrassed about. The Good News is true.

I might still be embarrassed, though, if the Good News weren't effective—if it didn't work. From free speech platforms on college campuses to pulpits in church services I have continually said, "Try it. Go ahead, just try it." I can say that with such conviction because God's Word is good. The power of God is contained in the Gospel, so it needs no excuse, requires no apology, and results in no embarrassment. That's not to say there aren't people who embarrass me by what they say and do with the Gospel—there are. I try to stay far away from them; I don't want to be associated with them. But there's no need to be embarrassed about the Gospel I'm offering you and suggesting you offer the world. It works.

There's one other thing about the Good News that might cause me embarrassment. What if it weren't for everyone? I'd be embarrassed if it were just for the wealthy. I'd be embarrassed if it were just for the poor. I'd be embarrassed if it were just for certain nationalities, skin colors, backgrounds, social positions, or education levels. I'd be embarrassed if it were only for a select group, or even if it were for most but excluded a few. Paul assures us differently: "It is the power of God for salvation to everyone who believes, to the Jew first and also to the Greek" (1:16). No one is excluded. It's for everyone, it's true, it works, and it's super news; that's why we need the radical lifestyle called for by the Gospel.

The Result of a Radical Lifestyle

"For it is the power of God for salvation to everyone who believes." *Salvation* is the result.

Has anyone ever asked you whether you were saved? Where I come from, we were encouraged to ask strangers on the street, "Are you saved?" They'd look around and think, *From what? Did a flowerpot just miss falling on my head? Is there a fire somewhere? What imminent danger am I unaware of? What's going on here?*

That's why, when I hear the word *saved*, I cringe a little. I know what it means, but it makes me nervous because I know other people don't. Jesus does "save," but what does that mean? Most people don't have a clue. They associate it with a caricature or character they've encountered.

Salvation is a word that means healing, wholeness. It's the

New Testament equivalent of the Old Testament *shalom*, which means to be filled with healing and peaceful rest. But more than lack of sickness and struggle, it means being filled with good things—infused with life. That's salvation.

There are two phases to salvation. The first comes with the law that's set down in Scripture, the moral Law of God that says, "This is what you should be doing." As I look at what the Law says I *should* be doing, and compare it to what I *am* doing, it gets my attention. That's what it's there for, to wake me up and make me aware. When I finally face my inability to keep God's Law, I have to accept the fact that it's impossible for me to keep. I can't get near it. I can't even come close.

As I fumble and fail in my attempt to keep God's Law, I am driven to the second phase of salvation—a love/trust relationship with God. I freely admit, "God, I can't do it on my own. I can't keep Your Law. I need You for healing and wholeness and life."

I've noticed a lot of people—and groups—never get to the second phase of a love/trust relationship. Their Christianity is confined to a code of morality; it's limited to the Law, to a list of do's and don'ts. That's not salvation; that's slavery.

When I first encountered a list of do's and don'ts, I quickly realized they could become goals in life. You can't keep them anyway, so why shackle yourself with them? True salvation sets you free; it saves you from yourself. For no matter how sharp, smart, or successful you are, when you come before God you realize you cannot keep His standard. When you realize that you stand before Him, you come to the point of saying, "OK, I give. I accept Your forgiveness for my failure to keep the Law by accepting Your payment and the relationship You offer me." That's true salvation.

The Law involves knowing *about* God; a love/trust relationship involves *knowing* God. Without a love/trust relationship you don't experience faith, prayer, the gifts, or God's power in your life, because you're still playing with a list of what Christians ought and ought not to do. Christianity is not a code, a cause, an ideology, or a program; it's a Person. It's also not simply another place to go on Sunday morning; it's a community in which to live. And, yes, Christianity is not just another religion—it's a radical lifestyle.

TWO FACTORS OF SALVATION

I've been a believer for over thirty years now. Until about seven years ago I thought salvation was only my relationship with God, my unity with Him. I didn't understand there are two factors of salvation—of the radical lifestyle—and they come as a package deal. I'm still trying to implement them, but now I know they must go together. Salvation means both unity with God—my relationship with Him, *and* community with people—my relationship with others. I realize you could be dying on a desert island and trust in Christ, therefore having unity with Him but not community with others. I'm sure in that case you would still get to heaven, but I'm also sure that that situation is the exception.

Most of us have the opportunity to experience both unity and community. Salvation is a radical lifestyle that requires both factors. Frankly, I'm tired of seeing people who are spiritually crippled and deformed because they only have unity with God and not community with people. Both are necessary for the healing and wholeness that salvation promises.

In the Gospel, "the righteousness of God is revealed from faith to faith; as it is written, 'But the righteous man shall live by faith'" (1:17). The righteousness of God breaks through by faith, for faith. *By* faith in Him we allow Him to break into our lives with His character and we accept Him by faith; *for* faith we allow others to be part of our lives and we care for them as He has cared for us.

THE REQUIREMENT FOR A RADICAL LIFESTYLE

We've seen that the reason for a radical lifestyle is that there's super news—Gospel. The result of a radical lifestyle is salvation. Now we come to the requirement of a radical lifestyle— believe it!

Maybe you've heard you must believe, *plus* take the sacraments, be born again in the right way, be baptized, or do this or that. Maybe you've heard there are things you mustn't do—no movies, drinking, dancing, or having fun. It's easy to complicate things. The Word simplifies things—just believe. The righteous man shall live and enjoy life, be excited and exhilarated with it—by faith.

In order to get this salvation, this Good News, it's necessary to go through something I call the ABCs of salvation. Both believers and nonbelievers need to ask, believe, and celebrate to make the transition from the Law to a love/trust relationship with God.

A: Ask for it. Asking involves saying "Help!" to God. We usually wait until He's gotten our attention before we do this. We ask when we're flat on our backs in the hospital; when our businesses are about to go under; when we're successful and soaring and we're not sure we know how to fly after all; when our relationships are falling apart; when our children are going berserk; etc. Saying "Help!" doesn't really change anything or get you anywhere in itself. It doesn't infuse you with the power of God, nor does it give you power to infuse others with. But asking is the beginning.

B: Believe in it. Maybe you've asked, then gone on to believe. You have God in your life. You have a relationship with Him, yet you're not appropriating His power. You've tried it and decided to join; you've made your reservation and have a guaranteed seat, but you're not living in the power of God. Your lifestyle and your Christianity aren't radical. Believing is necessary, but it isn't all there is. It's only the bridge to what comes next.

C: Celebrate it. It's easy to become so busy with asking and believing that we never get around to celebrating. We just ask more—"God, please help me"—and we try to believe more, "really" believe. We read our Bibles every day, we memorize Scripture, we go to prayer meetings, and we keep *doing* more because we have no idea when we've done enough to say that we "really" believe.

We don't need *more*. We need to move on to *celebrating*. Celebrating is living in the power of God. It's praising God for His power when you're making decisions, and thanking Him for His wisdom. It's a conscious activity of the mind, acknowledging God's presence and His enabling power to live the Christian life.

How can salvation be as simple as ABC? There are a lot of things about God I don't understand, but there are some things I do know. It's like what I know about the sun. Every day the sun rises; I know it's there and it's good. I know, but not because I can see it—I'd go blind if I looked directly at it for thirty seconds. I know, but not because I understand it—physics and I never did get along. I just know it's there and it's good because it sheds light on everything, making sense of the world around me.

It's the same with God. I know He's there and He's good, not because I can see Him or completely understand Him, but because the light He sheds puts all the pieces of the puzzle together for me in the very best way. It makes life livable; it makes it work.

The little chorus we teach our children to help them learn the alphabet ends with, "Now I've said my ABCs." We need to begin with the ABCs of salvation—*now*. "Behold now is 'the acceptable time,' behold now is 'the day of salvation'" (2 Cor. 6:2). A radical Christian lifestyle is living in the power of God *now*. We only have to ask for it, believe in it, and celebrate it!

We need the sense of urgency displayed by a man who was sentenced to die. Without mincing words, he wrote the following letter. "Dear Governor: They're going to hang me on Friday and today's Tuesday. Please do something—now!'

Christianity is not a "someday" thing. It's not just another religion. It's a radical lifestyle that requires you to live in the power of God, in unity with Him and in community with other people. It's true and it works. Now *that's* "rad"!

TWO

THE SKIN OF A REASON
STUFFED WITH A LIE

ost of us have an endless supply of them. At an instant's notice we can come up with one or more for even the most inauspicious occasion. We're pros at making them, and polished when doling them out. When we give one we sense relief, but when we get one we usually see it for what it is and call it by name. It's the skin of a reason stuffed with a lie. It's an excuse.

Perhaps the most classic excuse is given by one spouse when the other wants to make love: "I have a headache." There are lots of others to choose from in this situation, of course, including "I'm too tired," "It's too late," "It's too hot," "The neighbors will hear."

It's so much easier to avoid the truth by making an excuse than to admit it. We're like the mouse who, when encountered by an elephant for the first time, was asked, "What in the world happened to you? You're so puny!" Not wanting to admit he was only a mouse, the little creature made an excuse: "Well, I've been sick."

There's a bumper sticker that says, "If you feel far from God, who moved?" Good question, and Romans answers it for us. When you feel far from God, no matter what excuses you come up with, it's not because God moved—it's because *you* moved! Romans 1:18—3:20 talks about the distance that exists between man and God and the despair man feels because of it.

WITHOUT EXCUSE

Man has a problem, the same one he's had all along. His problem is that he's not getting any better. He may be getting smarter, more efficient, more advanced technologically; he may be seeing increases in gross national product and life expectancy, but he's not living life any more meaningfully or treating his fellow man any better. Everett Dirksen poignantly expressed it this way: "If we all woke up one morning the same race, the same color, and the same creed, by noon we'd find something to be prejudiced against."

There is something inside us that alienates us from God. There is also a vacuum inside us, and no matter what we put in it or how full we fill it, we still experience the same feelings of emptiness and alienation. It doesn't matter whether we're on the partial or prejudiced side, whether we have or have not; the same feelings are there. Believers as well as nonbelievers can feel far from God. Why?

It isn't because God is hiding. "The righteousness of God is revealed" (Rom. 1:17), or has broken through. But something else has also broken through:

The wrath of God is revealed from heaven against all ungodliness and unrighteousness of men, who suppress the truth in unrighteousness, because that which is known about God is evident within them; for God made it evident to them. For since the creation of the world His invisible attributes, His eternal power and divine nature, have been clearly seen, being understood through what has been made, so that they are without excuse (1:18-20).

God's wrath has broken through because the righteousness He revealed has been rejected. Even though God has given man natural lights to reveal His character, man chooses to suppress the truth in unrighteousness. Look at the way most people get along just fine without God—at least until they face a tragedy. Then they cry out for help. After God has gotten them through the crisis they say, "Thanks a lot, God. I'll see You at the next tragedy." God wants man to "see" Him all the time, and that's why He gave him two natural lights.

The first natural light is the one God has put within us. "That which is known about God is evident within them" (1:19). There is something about the way God created man that enables him to intrinsically know right from wrong. He carries moral principle, and when he violates it he experiences feelings of guilt. There are people who have hardened their consciences to such an extent that they no longer feel guilty, but everyone is born with a moral principle that tells him what's right and wrong. I call this first light conscience.

The second natural light is creation. "For since the creation of the world His invisible attributes, His eternal power and divine nature, have been clearly seen, being understood through what has been made" (1:20). As we look around at the trees, flowers, sky, oceans, and mountains, the second light shows us there must be Someone greater than ourselves. Even evolutionists are beginning to recognize some problems with their theory; no matter how much searching they do, they can't explain the physical universe. That's because God created everything. So we have two natural lights, conscience and creation.

THE GENTILE'S EXCUSE

Starting in verse 21, Paul talks about the excuses people make for not relating to God. He breaks these people into three groups. The first group is the Gentiles: "For even though they knew God, they did not honor Him as God, or give thanks;

but they became futile in their speculations, and their foolish heart was darkened" (1:21).

While at the American University in Washington, D.C. several years ago, I saw a young man sitting under a tree. He was staring intently at its branches and rocking back and forth with his hands folded in his lap. Curious as to what he was doing, I went over and sat next to him. I introduced myself, then asked, "What's your name?" After he told me, I said, "Do you mind if I ask what you're doing?"

"Not at all," he replied. "I'm worshiping."

"Really," I said. "God?"

"Oh, no." He shook his head. "The tree."

"This tree?" I asked, pointing up at it.

"Yeah, this tree," he said.

"What about all these other trees?" I asked. "Do you ever worship them?"

"No," he said emphatically. "Only *this* tree is worthy of worship."

At that point I excused myself. Futile speculations and a foolish heart indeed! But before you laugh at the guy under the tree, take a good look at yourself. What do you worship? Your dog, your cat, your car, your company, your mate, your kids? "Professing to be wise, they became fools, and exchanged the glory of the incorruptible God for . . . four-footed animals and crawling creatures" (1:22-23). What Paul is saying is that man put something else in the place of God. Man worshiped and served the creature rather than the Creator. His relationship with God was blurred.

The Gentile's excuse for not relating to God is that he has created his own god. "For this reason God gave them over to degrading passions; for their women exchanged the natural function for that which is unnatural, and in the same way also the men abandoned the natural function of the woman and burned in their desire toward one another, men with men committing indecent acts and receiving in their own persons the due penalty of their error" (1:26-27).

When there is no longer any difference between a man and a woman, society tends to disintegrate. When you don't have a relationship with God, your relationship with your-self—with your sexual self—becomes blurred.

Once your relationships with God and yourself have been blurred, you begin to experience difficulty relating to those around you. Paul gives us a long list of some of these difficulties:

> And just as they did not see fit to acknowledge God any longer, God gave them over to a depraved mind, to do those things which are not proper, being filled with all unrighteousness, wickedness, greed, malice; full of envy, murder, strife, deceit, malice; they are gossips, slanderers, haters of God, insolent, arrogant, boastful, inventors of evil, disobedient to parents, without understanding, untrustworthy, unloving, un-merciful; and, although they know the ordinance of God, that those who practice such things are worthy of death, they not only do the same, but also give hearty approval to those who practice them (1:28-31).

I doubt Paul missed anyone with his extensive list. We all have trouble relating to our neighbors. It's a natural progres-sion from a blurred relationship with God to a blurred rela-tionship with self to a blurred relationship with your neigh-bor. And it's all because people try to excuse themselves from relating to God.

THE MORALIST'S EXCUSE

The Gentile's excuse is he has created his own God. The moralist, meanwhile, excuses himself by *playing* God:

> Therefore you are without excuse, every man of you who passes judgment, for in that you judge another, you condemn yourself; for you who judge practice the same things. And we know that the judgment of God

rightly falls upon those who practice such things. And do you suppose this, O man, when you pass judgment upon those who practice such things and do the same yourself, that you will escape the judgment of God? Or do you think lightly of the riches of His kindness and forbearance and patience, not knowing that the kindness of God leads you to repentance? But because of your stubbornness and unrepentant heart you are storing up wrath for yourself in the day of wrath and revelation of the righteous judgment of God, who will render to every man according to his deeds: to those who by perseverance in doing good seek for glory and honor and immortality, eternal life; but to those who are selfishly ambitious and do not obey the truth, but obey unrighteousness, wrath and indignation (2:1-8).

The moralist is the person who continually pontificates. His two favorite words are should and ought, and he has an ample supply of them for everyone: "You shouldn't drink—in fact, you shouldn't even go into a place that serves liquor. Actually, you shouldn't even smell the stuff!" The interesting thing is that the Bible doesn't forbid drinking. But the moralist seems so "together" that surely he *must* know.

The moralist sees himself as clergy working undercover as a layman. He's memorized all the best "should" and "ought" verses and recites them prolifically. The interesting thing about the moralist is that he's often guilty of the very "sin" he's pontificating about. There are countless examples in our society, many of which I encounter in counseling. When people continually speak against something, they are usually speaking to themselves to prevent some undesired behavior.

The moralist believes God grades on the curve—that if he can do more good than bad, everything will balance out in the end. The problem is that God doesn't even give grades. Everything is pass/fail with Him.

THE JEW'S EXCUSE

I have a Jewish friend whose grandfather was a rabbi. When his grandfather was 13, he was given an unbelievable examination. A spike was driven through the first five books of the Old Testament, and he had to recite every word the spike touched on every page—in order—in all five books! And he did it—because he had memorized it, word for word.

The Jew or the Christian who knows the Bible without really knowing God can easily say, "Hey, I'm a member. I've got my card right here to prove it. It says, 'I know the Word' on the front, and on the back it says, 'I study it and store it up.'" What he can't honestly say is that God acknowledges his membership. He's carrying a counterfeit card and offering the excuse of "membership" to keep from relating to God.

Paul puts it this way in 2:17-21:

But if you bear the name "Jew," and rely upon the Law, and boast in God, and know His will, and approve the things that are essential, being instructed out of the Law, and are confident that you yourself are a guide to the blind, a light to those who are in darkness, a corrector of the foolish, a teacher of the immature, having in the Law the embodiment of knowledge and of the truth, you, therefore, who teach another, do you not teach yourself? You who preach that one should not steal, do you steal?

The apostle sums the matter up with verse 25: "For indeed circumcision is of value, if you practice the Law; but if you are a transgressor of the Law, your circumcision has become uncircumcision." You may be a card-carrying Bible whiz, but even people who have learned the Law well on their own can't keep it very well on their own. It doesn't make any difference if you have the Bible or even if you have it all memorized; you can still be far from God because you can't make it on your own.

Look at 3:10-20 for proof:

> There is none righteous, not even one; there is none
> who understands, there is none who seeks for God; all
> have turned aside, together they have become useless;
> there is none who does good, there is not even one.
> Their throat is an open grave, with their tongues they
> kept deceiving, the poison of asps is under their lips;
> whose mouth is full of cursing and bitterness; their
> feet are swift to shed blood, destruction and misery
> are in their paths, and the path of peace have they not
> known. There is no fear of God before their eyes.
>
> Now we know that whatever the Law says, it
> speaks to those who are under the Law, that every
> mouth may be closed, and all the world may become
> accountable to God; because by the works of the Law
> no flesh will be justified in His sight; for through the
> Law comes the knowledge of sin.

Paul is saying here that knowledge of the Law is not a
membership card, but rather a mirror to show us what God's
standard is and where we fall short. "For all have sinned and
fall short of the glory of God" (v. 23). It's not an excuse for
being far from God, for not relating with Him; it's an ac-
knowledgment of our total need for God.

LOST AT SEA

Earl Palmer, a pastor of a Presbyterian church in Berkeley,
California illustrates this part of Romans with the following
parable:

Four people were on a cruise from Los Angeles to Ha-
waii. After dinner, when they were about a thousand miles
out, a friend asked, "Can I take your picture together up on
the deck?"

"Sure," came the enthusiastic reply, and they all proceeded
to the deck to pose. The photographer had them stand right
in front of the side railing.

As he was getting ready to take the picture he said, "Would you mind moving back just a little bit? I'm having trouble focusing." Not knowing that the photographer had loosened the railing behind them, the innocent foursome followed his instruction.

"I'm still having a little trouble," the photographer said. "Could you back up a couple more steps?" You guessed it—with a splash all four of them went overboard. The photographer waved good-bye to them and headed back downstairs. Some friend! But that was the least of their worries now. With a thousand miles separating them from either shore, the four floating passengers had a serious problem.

One of the overboard passengers was an idol worshiper. Fortunately for him he had his idol with him at dinner, on deck, and now down in the water. It weighed thirty-nine pounds, but the man was thankful to have it in his moment of need. He began to stroke the nose of the idol three times in a northward direction and then prayed to the idol. Certainly that would get him out of deep water, he thought. But for some reason it didn't work. As he stroked and prayed and stroked and prayed, the idol got heavier and heavier. His bobbling began to resemble sinking, and he decided it was time to drop the idol. It wasn't doing the job.

The second overboard passenger, a moralist, was a specimen of physical fitness. Every morning at 6 he had gone down to the gym to swim two miles and strut his rippling muscles around for all to see. He wasn't at all concerned about being dumped in the ocean—in fact he was downright obnoxious about it. "Didn't I warn you guys?" he said to the others. "I've been telling you for years to eat right and exercise; but no, you wouldn't listen. Now there's no way you're going to make it to shore. But just in case you care to try, the side-stroke works best for long distances." Poor guy, he didn't realize how far a thousand miles is. He actually thought he could swim to shore—at least for the first few miles. . . .

Overboard passenger number three was a legalist. He

dealt with the situation quite logically. He knew they were a thousand miles from either shore and that the situation was desperate. There was no way of swimming the distance and no chance of rescue. It would be either drowning or shark-bait time for all of them. "I told you that photographer couldn't be trusted," the legalist said. "But you were all so vain you had to have your picture taken. I knew something awful would occur if we went up on deck with him. I just knew something like this would happen." And down he went, knowing full well why.

The last of the four overboard passengers was an existen-tialist. He didn't take things too seriously. To him the past was the past and the future was the future; all that concerned him was the present. Life only had meaning in the moment it was lived, so he wasn't worried about his destiny. He would just tread water, soak it in, and eventually sink.

That's man's predicament. He's lost at sea with no life jacket, no raft, and no Coast Guard to come along and rescue him. All he can do is swim, and that only for a short time. He can't make it on his own; he needs help. He needs a big bridge to get him to shore. That's what Christianity is all about, and that's what God provides. Radical Christianity says there's no excuse for being far from God, because God provides the forgiveness to get us back to shore.

MAKING THE TRADE

The only way to keep from sinking is to stop living your life without God. I've heard thousands of excuses for not relating to God, and none of them works. Only forgiveness helps. You can excuse your life away or exchange your life with God for a new one. It's your choice.

In one hand you have a death certificate, because you're out in the middle of the ocean with no way to get back to shore. In the other hand you have God and His Son and eternal life. All God wants you to do is exchange with Him—

make a trade. You don't have to follow forty-nine steps, stare at stained glass, memorize the first five books of the Bible, or say the Doxology backward. All you have to do is make the exchange, and once you realize you're out of excuses, you'll be ready to make the trade.

An extremely wealthy man was talking to his future son-in-law. "If I give you this big dowry when you marry my daughter," he asked, "what will you give me in return?" The future son-in-law, who didn't have anything, stood silent for a moment and then said sheepishly, "How about a receipt?" When you realize there is no excuse for being far from God, for not relating to Him, and you exchange your life for His life, all you can do is accept it and say, "Thank you for the gift!"

That's not to say that rescue requires *nothing* of the rescuee. A man had fallen in love with the girl he was dating. One evening they were out in a rowboat. Not knowing it was dangerous, the girl stood up to see something. "Sweetheart," the man cried, "don't stand up or you'll. . . ." It was too late. She fell in. She couldn't swim and she started to panic. He reached out and grabbed her hair—which turned out to be a wig. Then he got hold of her left arm—an artificial one that came off in his hand. "Listen, Sweetheart," he said. "If I'm going to help you, you've got to give me something I can hang onto!"

That's the way God puts it to you. If you want Him to help you, you have to stop giving Him puny excuses and start offering Him something He can hang onto—namely, recognition of your inability to save yourself.

Don't excuse your life away—exchange it with God for the life He gives. It's the only thing that works, and it's for believers as well as nonbelievers. I've found it's easy for me to go sailing along without continually living the exchanged life, to stop counting on Him and try to live in my own strength—and ultimate death. You may have been a believer for a long time, you may know the Bible inside and out, and you may even be a fabulous speaker or teacher. But God is not interested in your list. He wants your life. All He needs is a little cooperation from you. Don't excuse your life away—exchange your life with God.

THREE
THE CLEAN
SLATE CLUB

M an is in a predicament, and the only thing that can rescue him is the power of God. Actually, it's much more than a momentary rescue—it's a complete, permanent reversal. God doesn't just throw us a life jacket, drop us a rowboat and a couple of oars, or even take us on board and get us to the nearest shore. He gives us life where there is no life, forever. No matter what we've done in the past, are doing in the present, or are planning to do in the future, God—by His power—reverses our predicament. All we have to do is tap into His power.

In the fifth chapter of Romans, Paul talks about two Adams.

Therefore, just as through one man sin entered into the world, and death through sin, and so death spread to all men, because all sinned--for until the Law sin was in the world; but sin is not imputed when there is no law. Nevertheless death reigned from Adam until Moses, even over those who had not sinned in the likeness of Adam's offense, who is a type of Him who was to come (5:12-14).

Paul uses a word here that some people avoid like the plague. It makes them uneasy, it embarrasses them, and at times it even frightens them. The word is *sin*, a simple word describing something we are often blind to recognize and that always blocks us from receiving God's power.

Sin is basically self-centered rebellion. It's saying to God, "God, You go Your way and I'll go mine. Check with me when I'm seventy-two or seventy-three and we'll negotiate a deal then. We could work a deal now, but I'd rather do it later." Sin is living your life without God, exchanging the true God for another god, creating your own god. It's being unwilling to receive God's love and love Him as well as being unwilling to love and receive love from others.

WE ARE IN ADAM

"Through one man sin entered into the world, and death through sin, and so death spread to all men, because all sinned" (5:12). Because of our self-centered rebellion, we are all condemned to die. Because of our attitude of indifference and disobedience to God, we are all sentenced to death.

The reason is twofold. One is that Adam sinned, and as members of the human race we are all part of him. We have descended from him and are therefore connected to him. In a sense we are all part of the first fall of man back in the Garden of Eden, where Adam and Eve rebelled against God.

The second reason for our death sentence is at the end of verse 12: "because all sinned." Not only are we connected to Adam in his fall; we have also fallen individually. Each of us has sinned by rebelling against God.

Jesus emphasized this over and over again to the Pharisees, who tended to exclude themselves from the rest of fallen man. The Pharisees were pompous and proud. They had it all together, and they sported the religious robes, heavenly air, and stained-glass voices to prove it. They looked great on the outside, but Jesus saw through their sinless appearance to their sinful hearts. He told them that hating is as bad as murdering, and coveting a woman is the same as committing adultery (Matt. 5:21-28). Jesus knew the Pharisees were in the same predicament as everyone else, because all have sinned.

Because we have sinned and are part of the fallen human race, we can't get to God on our own no matter what we try. Some people say, "If you join our church and believe as we do, you'll get there," but no matter what church you join or what doctrine you defend, it's not going to make any difference. What you believe and how you relate to God *will* make a difference.

Religion says you can get to God on your own. It sets out a system of do's and don'ts, shoulds and shouldn'ts. You've got to do this and you mustn't do that; then you can get to God. Man tries to jump the chasm that exists between him and God, but he doesn't get very far. Even building bridges doesn't work because the chasm is so great. All the "shoulds" in the world can't span the distance.

As we've already seen, Christianity is not a religion, it's a relationship. Christianity says you can't get to God on your own. But because man is unable to reach across the chasm, God reaches out to man. God provides the bridge whereby man can have a relationship with Him. Man's predicament of being out in the ocean a thousand miles from either shore is thus reversed.

WE ARE IN CHRIST

The reversal is described in 5:15-19:

> For if by the transgression of the one the many died, much more did the grace of God and the gift by the grace of the one Man, Jesus Christ, abound to the many. And the gift is not like that which came through the one who sinned; for on the one hand the judgment arose from one transgression resulting in

condemnation, but on the other hand the free gift arose from many trangressions resulting in justification. For if by the transgression of the one, death reigned through the one, much more those who receive the abundance of grace and of the gift of righteousness will reign in life through the One, Jesus Christ. So then as through one transgression there resulted condemnation to all men, even so through one act of righteousness there resulted justification of life to all men. For as through the one man's disobedience the many were made sinners, even so through the obedience of the One the many will be made righteous.

God demands a payment—a death payment—for our sins, whether or not we're aware of our rebellion. "For until the Law sin was in the world; but sin is not imputed when there is no law" (5:13). Even if sin is not measured, we feel the consequences when we disobey God. If you neglect or ignore your family, your family is going to fall apart. If you exchange God for other gods, you won't be able to relate to Him.

Whether there's a law or not, you are still separated from God, have still disobeyed Him, and are still guilty before Him. When God's principles are violated, He demands that the price be paid. He demands an Adam, a perfect Adam, to come and pay for the sins of the imperfect Adamic race. You can pay by dying for an eternity, or you can accept God's payment by the death of the second Adam, Jesus Christ. Because the first Adam failed, God provided a second Adam. In the first Adam we are in a predicament. In the last Adam we are given a bridge to relate to God.

RESULTS OF A RELATIONSHIP WITH CHRIST

Earlier in chapter 5 Paul lists seven things we receive when we come into a relationship with the second Adam. We came into a relationship with the first Adam automatically as his children. C.S. Lewis writes of that relationship in the creative and captivating *Chronicles of Narnia*. In a land of excitement and enchantment in which animals speak, the two human children are always greeted with, "Are you the sons and daughters of Adam and Eve?" What the animals were asking is, "Are you in Adam?" All human beings are in the first Adam. And all human beings have the opportunity to be in the second Adam—Jesus Christ.

The first thing we receive when we come into a relationship with Christ is listed in 5:1: "Therefore having been justified by faith, we have peace with God through our Lord Jesus Christ." When we come into a relationship with Christ, God gives us peace. But notice that we cannot have the peace *of* God until we have peace *with* God.

The second benefit of a relationship with Christ, Paul says, is being introduced to God. "Through whom also we have obtained our introduction by faith into this grace in which we stand" (5:2). Often in order to meet a powerful or influential person you must know someone who can introduce you. If you want to meet the Pope, for instance, you need someone who can arrange for you to see him. The same holds true for meeting the President of the United States. Not long ago a friend said to me, "I know President Reagan pretty well, and if you'd like to meet him I'll arrange something the next time he's in town."

"W-what would I say?" I stammered.

"It doesn't matter," my friend said. "Just meet with him. I can get you in to meet with him."

Over the years I've heard that a lot. Somebody always knows some important person and "can get you right in." Sometimes he can; sometimes he can't. Christ can definitely get us in to see God. He is our introduction to the Father. When we are in Christ we have an automatic and immediate audience with God.

Paul says the third benefit we receive is hope—hope for the future, hope for the glory of God. "And we exult in hope of the glory of God" (5:2). Verse 3 mentions the fourth benefit: "And not only this, but we also exult in our tribulations." In the midst of our tribulations, if we have a relationship with God, we can still experience joy.

That doesn't mean you say, "Oh, praise the Lord, my husband has cancer," or "It's just wonderful, our business has gone under and we're going to lose everything." That's nuts! It does mean you can experience an unusual joy, even in the midst of trials, because you have the peace of God. You have been introduced to Him, and you have hope that you're going to get through. That's a major difference between a believer and a nonbeliever. A nonbeliever isn't sure he's going to get through it, but a believer has the hope that he will. That's something to rejoice about!

The fifth benefit is in 5:5: "And hope does not disappoint, because the love of God has been poured out within our hearts." When we come into a relationship with Christ, God pours out His love into our hearts with the intention that we will then pour it out to others. Every human being has an incredible, unbelievable need to be loved, just as they are and for who they are. I need to be loved that way, and so do you. That's how God loves us, and that's how He wants us to love others.

Back in chapter 1, Paul said that the wrath of God has been revealed. In 5:9 he says, "Much more then, having now been justified by His blood, we shall be saved from the wrath of God through Him." That's the sixth thing we receive from our relationship with Christ: salvation from God's wrath. Christ interceded on our behalf and bore the punishment that was rightfully ours.

Finally, in 5:11 we have the seventh benefit: "And not only this, but we also exult in God through our Lord Jesus Christ, through whom we have now received the reconciliation." We are now acceptable to God. We measure up to His standard because of our relationship with Christ. Chapters 3 and 4 explain in detail that the only way we are reconciled is through faith. Just as Abraham believed the Word of God and it was accounted to him as righteousness, so we too must exercise faith in order to come into a relationship with Christ.

WE ARE JUSTIFIED BY FAITH

Paul uses the word *justified* throughout chapters 3 and 4 and again in the beginning of chapter 5: "Therefore having been justified by faith, we have peace with God through our Lord Jesus Christ" (5:1). Justification is a theological term that means to be declared righteous. When you come into a relationship with Christ, God by His power reverses your predicament and declares you righteous. In addition, every time you blow it He sends another bucket of grace and pours it all over you. Justification means "just as if you've never sinned." Can you believe that's how God looks at you?

I have a hard time believing God could forgive some people I know. I have an even harder time believing He could forgive *me!* But He does. God cleans your slate and you become a member of the Clean Slate Club when you come into a relationship with Him. When God looks at my name He says, "OK, where's Howard?" (When people are serious they call me Howard and God is serious!) "What's his slate look like? Is it clean?" And the on-duty angel reports back, "Timmons is clean. We's wiped up slicker than a whistle." Now, I know there are lots of people who can see some marks from where they're sitting; but from God's perspective my slate's clean.

After God wipes our slates clean, He does something that's even more exciting. From 1 John 1:9 we learn, "If we confess [or agree with God] our sins [the things we do that don't follow His principles], He is faithful and righteous to forgive us our sins and to cleanse us from all unrighteousness" (brackets added). In other words, He keeps on wiping our slates clean. Our predicament is overwhelming, but the power of God is even more so.

WE ARE TO BOW TWICE

The person who has influenced me more than anyone else is Francis Schaeffer. From his study center in Huemoz, Switzerland, philosopher and theologian Schaeffer challenged people to think and take action concerning their Christianity. He said Christianity comes down to this: Every person must bow his or her knee twice.

The first bending of the knee is before the first Adam. It's bowing in humble admission of man's predicament and admitting, "I'm in a mess, God. I'm a thousand miles from shore and there's no way back." The first bowing acknowledges man's crisis.

That's why I have such complete confidence in talking to anyone on earth. I know other people are just like me. I don't care who they are, where they live, what kind of car they drive, or how much money they have in the bank. I know they're in the same predicament I'm in. When life brings us to the deathbed, everything balances out. All of a sudden everyone's equal. I'm amazed at how many calls I get from people who never wanted to talk before, but in the face of crisis, they decide it's time. The crisis of man is a great equalizer.

Schaeffer said we shouldn't be surprised at the crisis of man. We shouldn't be surprised when we hear about a murder, rape, burglary, or the tragedies in Lebanon. We shouldn't be surprised that man messes up, because man is in a predicament. He's a thousand miles from shore, and without God he's in a lot of trouble.

The second bending of the knee is before the second Adam, Jesus Christ. We do that when we realize who He is and how His sacrifice, love, and power redeem us from our predicament.

GOD'S POWER, GOD'S LOVE

The Christian knows the mess that man is in and the power and love of God. God doesn't love us *because* we have faith in

Him. There's no way we could ever muster up enough faith to make Him love us. God loves us because He chooses to, just as we are, and no matter what we do in the next few days or weeks or years He loves us just the same. Our faith simply allows us to plug into God's love and receive it, and that's what the Christian is all about. He's joined the Clean Slate Club by coming into a personal relationship with God. He's reversed the predicament he's in; he's not treading water any more.

Bill Cosby, my favorite comedian, tells a pertinent story about Noah and God. In it God says to Noah, "Noah!"

"W-what God, what now?" Noah answers.

"You know those two hippopotamuses you've got down there in the bottom of the ark?"

"Yeah, I know," says Noah.

"Well, both of them are male. That won't work, Noah. So I want you to go down and take one of them out and go get a female to replace him."

Now, Noah is beat beyond belief. He is totally wiped out, and in order to get a male out and a female back in he would have to take out all the other animals that came in after the hippos.

"God," Noah says, "You know how tired I am. You're God; change one of the males into a female."

"Noah," God replies, "I want you to do what I've asked, for Me."

"Oh, come on, God," Noah pleads, "You change him. You can do it."

"Noah," God says in closing, "let Me put it this way. How long can you tread water?"

That's the question I want you to ask yourself. How long can you tread water? You're a thousand miles from shore, and there's no way to get there except through the power of God.

It works something like this. In one hand, on a pad of paper, you have all the sins you have ever committed, and God says that those sins, that disobedience, that rebellion against Him must be paid for by death. Either you can die for an eternity, which is a very long time, or you can accept the death of God's Son on the cross for you.

What God wants you to do, and what you must do in order to get into the Clean Slate Club, is to realize you cannot pay for your sins on your own. It's impossible. The crisis is too great; you can't swim that far and you can't tread water that long. Transfer your sins to the other hand and give them to the only One who can pay for them—by accepting God's power and payment through Christ's death on the cross. Admit that there's no way out of your predicament and submit to the love of God.

Christ said He would pay for all your sins, down to the last scribble on the last line of the last piece of paper in your pad—past, present, and future. He paid for them all on the cross. All you have to do is accept His payment. If you receive His gift, you are justified and declared righteous and inherit eternal life. If you refuse His gift, you are left to "tread water."

You can receive God's gift by accepting Jesus Christ's death payment for you, by realizing you're in a predicament and recognizing God's power as the only possibility for reversal. If you have never asked God to come into your life, you can do it now through prayer. There is no set formula to follow, and there is nothing magical about the words. Prayer is simply talking to God. God is reaching out to you and wants you to relate to Him. If you are tired of treading water and want a relationship with God, pray this kind of prayer to God, and become a member of the Clean Slate Club:

Dear God, I realize I have sinned against You and cannot pay for this sin on my own. I accept Jesus Christ's payment for me. Thank You for Your power that reverses my predicament. Amen.

FOUR
I GOT MY ACT TOGETHER BUT FORGOT WHERE I PUT IT

*P*eople everywhere are struggling with identity crises, trying to figure out, "Who am I?" and "What am I all about?" When they finally get some answers, they realize they aren't nearly as wonderful as they thought they were, and the world doesn't revolve around them after all. At that point they start searching for painkillers that offer temporary relief from their desperation. Even Christians, if they're honest, will tell you that the longer they're Christians the more inadequate they realize they are.

The problem gets worse when we're attacked by what I call an anti-human bombardment. So much of what we hear on a daily, consistent basis is in anti-human terms. We're told we have no unique dignity as human beings, for example. We hear it so often that even when we're told, "You're special," we don't believe it. As we begin to view ourselves as unimportant, our search for identity becomes even more desperate.

Some of us go in the other direction, deceiving ourselves into thinking we're a bit *bigger* than we are. We're like the mouse who, along with an elephant, crossed a bridge. As the two went over the bridge it shook like crazy and wobbled all

43

over the place. Even after they got to the other side, the bridge kept shaking. As they stood looking back, the mouse said, "Boy, *we* gave that bridge a scare, didn't we?"

A woodpecker had the same problem. He was chopping away at a big, old oak tree when a storm moved in. It began to thunder, but the woodpecker just kept pecking away. All of a sudden the tree was hit by lightning, cracked in two, and fell to the ground. The woodpecker flew away, thinking, "Hey, am I hot stuff or am I hot stuff?"

While we've been deceiving ourselves into thinking we're bigger than we are, other people are making us feel smaller than we are. Then we try to conform to the world's mold, and we become increasingly confused. These days we don't just try to keep up with the Joneses, but also the Smiths and the Johnsons and the Harrisons. There are so many people to keep up with, we don't know what or whom to use as a measuring stick.

So far in Romans we've seen that we're in a predicament. We're a thousand miles out in the middle of the ocean with no way to get to shore. Only God's power can rescue us, and He not only rescues us, but reverses our predicament. He justifies us, declares us righteous, and provides us with a bridge by sending Christ to pay for our sins. That's justification—our position with God. In the next chapter we'll look at sanctification—our process of growth with God, being set apart, maturing. But before we can grow with God, we have to be firmly planted. We have to be set in our position with Him and be secure in our identity.

ACCEPTING OUR POSITION

When you believe in Christ—when you accept His payment for your sins on the cross and come into a relationship with God—two dimensions of your life change. One is the spiritual dimension—the eternal side of your life, and the other is the earthly dimension—the temporal side of your life (see figure 1).

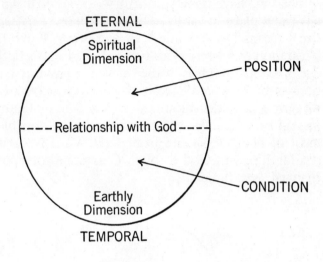

FIGURE 1

Above the horizontal line, in the spiritual dimension, is your position in Christ. Being "in Christ" means you are enveloped by Him—you are covered by and contained inside Him. When you express your desire for a relationship with God and put your faith in Him, He places you in Christ. Then, and this is the most incredible thing that happens, every time God looks at you He sees Christ! Because you are in Christ, God sees His Son when He looks at you.

When God punches me up on His heavenly computer and examines my "slate," He doesn't find anything. It's clean! Not because I haven't messed up and put marks on it, but because I am in Christ; therefore God sees His Son when He looks at me. The same thing is true of you if you are in Christ. God says you are blameless, without reproach, complete and perfect in Christ. It is truly incredible! It's not something we've made up in our heads or even something we hope for in the future. It is what *happens* when we are in Christ.

To be more specific, we are spiritually *baptized* into Christ. When we are baptized with water, it's a physical sign of what we have done spiritually—an outward sign of what has taken place inwardly. The Greek word *baptizō*, "to baptize," means "to dip into," as in dyeing. I like the classic illustration of a white cloth being dipped into a bucket of red dye. Once the cloth is in the bucket, it has a new identification—it becomes red instead of white. Once we are in Christ we have a new identification—we are seen by God as perfect instead of sinful. We are no longer in the horrible predicament of being separated from God. We have come into a relationship with God through Christ, and our position has changed (see figure 2).

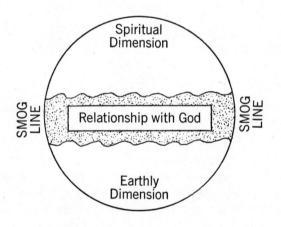

FIGURE 2

Between the spiritual and earthly dimensions is what I call the "smog line." It's there because there's still sin in the world, and when we sin we slip beneath it, blurring our relationship with God. It's not that we're no longer related to God when that happens; we're just not as close or enjoying it as much.

When I have a fight with my wife, for example, I don't go

to her afterward and say, "Now that we've had a fight, I need to ask you: Will you marry me?" I don't need to ask her to marry me again; we're already married. I need to admit that I blew it and ask her to forgive me. When I do, I move back up through the smog line and our relationship can continue to grow.

The same is true of our relationship with God. When we sin, we need to admit that we blew it and ask God to forgive us. Then our relationship with Him can continue to grow.

Our condition in our temporal lives is affected by our position in our spiritual lives. But—and I realize this is a radical statement—our position in our spiritual lives is not affected by our condition in our temporal lives. That is, no matter how badly you mess up down here, you cannot change your position once you are in Christ. Your condition can be affected by your position, but no condition can affect your position in Christ.

Paul says it this way:

What shall we say then? Are we to continue in sin that grace might increase? May it never be! How shall we who died to sin still live in it? Or do you not know that all of us who have been baptized into Christ Jesus have been baptized into His death? Therefore we have been buried with Him through baptism into death, in order that as Christ was raised from the dead through the glory of the Father, so we too might walk in newness of life. For if we have become united with Him in the likeness of His death, certainly we shall be also in the likeness of His resurrection (6:1-5).

Notice what Paul is saying here. He says that when we are baptized, two things happen. We are baptized or united with His death, and we are baptized or united with His resurrection.

Knowing this, that our old self [our old manner of life] was crucified with Him, that our body of sin might be done away with, that we should no longer be slaves to sin; for he who has died is freed from sin. Now if we have died with Christ, we believe that we shall also live with Him, knowing that Christ, having been raised from the dead, is never to die again; death no longer is master over Him. For the death that He died, He died to sin, once for all; but the life that He lives, He lives to God (6:6-10, brackets added).

Because of our baptism, our identification with Christ, we are no longer slaves to sin. Before we were in Christ we had to obey our master, sin, that self-centered rebellion that keeps us from God. Paul says we are freed from that slavery by death. Dying is the best way to get out of slavery, because once you're dead a master can't get you to do anything! It's an irrevocable principle of life that dead slaves don't do much. God has us die with Christ—be baptized into His death, in order that we may have life in Him—and be baptized into His resurrection. We are then dead to sin and alive to God.

THREE WORDS TO LIVE BY

There are three keys to accepting our position in Christ. The first one is *knowing*.

God wants us to *know* that sin is no longer master over us—that we are dead to sin and alive to God. Notice, however, that Paul doesn't say the *master* is dead. We still have a sin nature inside us that is constantly pulling us away from God. The master is still there; we just don't have to obey him anymore because we're no longer his slaves.

To put it another way: if you had been in jail for ten years, you would have grown accustomed to doing what the jailer told you. But once you were freed, you wouldn't have to listen to him anymore. You could ignore him when he came up to you on the street and said, "Hey, what are you doing out here? Get back in there!" You wouldn't have to do what he said because he wouldn't be your master anymore. You're dead to sin and alive to God.

The second key to accepting our position in Christ is found in 6:11: "Even so consider yourselves to be dead to sin, but alive to God in Christ Jesus." Or as the *King James Version* puts it, "Reckon . . . yourselves." It's the first major command in the Book of Romans: reckon yourselves, or consider yourselves, dead to sin and alive to God. What does that mean? God has just said through Paul that He wants us to know we're dead to sin and alive to God. Now He says *reckon* it—*count* on it to be true.

Knowing and reckoning are two different things. The following is a crude illustration, but it definitely makes its point. Say that someone is upset with me, or has just picked me at random in a crowd, and has stabbed me with a ballpoint pen. I know I have just been stabbed, so I say, "Hark, I have been stabbed with a ballpoint pen. It really hurts. Blood is gushing out of my body. I think I may die soon." I *know* I have just been stabbed. It's no big deal; I just *know* it.

Reckon is a different word. If I reckon, I say, "Hark, I have been stabbed with a ballpoint pen. It really hurts. Blood is gushing out of my body. I think I may die soon. *Help!*" The difference between *know* and *reckon* is *action*—doing something about it. God says, "Don't just know it; count on it to be true." If you are in Christ, in Him you *are* dead to sin and alive to God. *Reckoning* is the second key.

Verses 12-14 allude to *yielding*, which is the third key to accepting our position in Christ:

Therefore do not let sin reign in your mortal body that you should obey its lusts, and do not go on presenting the members of your body to sin as instruments of unrighteousness; but present yourselves to God as those alive from the dead, and your members as instruments of righteousness to God. For sin shall not be master over you, for you are not under law, but under grace.

There are two parts to presenting our bodies. The first part is to stop presenting our bodies to sin. The second is to start presenting them to God. We are to *quit* doing what we used to do and *start* doing what we ought to do. The problem is that a lot of us are caught up in conforming to the ways of other people. We go along with the crowd, do what people expect us to, and try to please everyone. In the process we never get anywhere. In Christ we don't have to be conformed; we can stand alone and be transformed. We can walk in "newness of life" (6:4).

I'm convinced that many people who are believers—probably most believers where I live—are not being transformed. Even though they are in Christ, they have not accepted their position by knowing, reckoning, and yielding. They're still struggling with their identities in Christ, trying to figure out how they fit in this world and living a roller-coaster lifestyle with poor self-images. They're still struggling with conformity, trying to keep up with the guy down the block, the lady one street over, or the family around the corner. They "need" that nicer car, fancier clothes, or bigger house.

No wonder they're trying to figure out what Christianity is all about. They've gotten their act together but then forgot where they put it—in Christ.

The antidote to conformity is to accept our position in Christ, to know that we're freed from sin and alive to God, to reckon it to be true, and to yield—to quit doing what we know is wrong and start doing what we know is right. It's that simple.

ACTING ON OUR POSITION

When we're trying to fit into a mold, usually making bad choices in the process, we lose our freedom. When we identify with Christ, we are freed from the rat race of conformity and can be transformed into the people God wants us to be.

I'm afraid most of us don't know who we are or what God intends us to be. We're not very happy with what we've got because we're not focusing on our position in Christ, on the fact that we are in Him. We're still being conformed, not transformed.

Social etiquette encourages us to inquire about people's well-being. Lately I've noticed when I ask people, "How are you?" they actually *tell* me. Often their stories are melodramas, tragedies, tales of desperation. People are talking about their problems because they're focused on their conditions. We all have our share of problems—I've got a few myself that I'm not very excited about—but the problems aren't the whole story.

I can tell you about my problems and how bad things are and how I'm trying to survive. But I want to tell you something else: I've got hope! I'm not caught up in my condition; I'm free because of my position in Christ. That doesn't mean I'm out of the rat race, but I am free to be transformed into the person God wants me to be. When I'm focused on my condition, even when things are going well, I become weak and vulnerable to every kind of problem there is.

THE POWER TO CHANGE

One result of focusing on our position in Christ is that we have the power to change. Everyone struggles with change. Some people want to change and others don't, but for those who *want* to there is power to do so. And much of the changing process has to do with the way we think.

I heard recently of a man whose finger was completely cut off. He took the severed finger, held it back in place on his hand, and started his mind working. He concentrated his thoughts and energy toward that finger, thinking positively about his injury. On his way to the hospital, that finger began to heal.

Usually when someone cuts a finger, not to mention cutting it off, he spews out a streak of profanity and then chides himself or whomever else was involved for being so stupid. His thinking is negative; he's convinced he's going to lose his finger. But this man thought positively and his finger began to heal. When the doctor examined the man's hand, he couldn't believe the finger had been completely cut off. God created our minds with incredible potential for change, but we have to input it properly and think positively.

THE POWER OVER DEATH

Another result of focusing on our position instead of our condition is that we realize Christ's power over death. When we are in Christ, death no longer has dominion over us.

The greatest problem people face today is figuring out how not to die. I'm trying to figure it out myself. I know when God's ready for me I'll go, but I don't want to write my own ticket.

We're trying to find out how not to die, how to get out of dying, how to get over death. In Christ, there is power over death—it is no longer master over us. It's still around, but it isn't the end. Death is not terminal—it's just a temporal experience through which we must pass.

THE POWER OF GOD

As a result of our position in Christ, there's power to change, power over death, and the ongoing power of God in our lives. Years ago a great evangelist said, "The world has yet to see a man or woman who is totally dependent upon God." God has made available to us all the power we need to live the Christian life, and He's waiting to give it to us. As we are baptized in Christ, identify with Him, and accept and act on our position in Him, we receive that power.

As we identify with Christ, we are given the power to survive our identity struggles and freed to be the people we are meant to be. Activating that power in our lives simply involves turning our lives over to Christ, getting into His

Word, and believing it.

Paul said to know it, count on it, and do it. It's as though you have a big checking account up in heaven, and while you're down on earth you can write checks on it. The money—God's power—is there, and because of your position in Christ all you have to do to get it is to write the checks.

A drunk man was driving down a one-way street against the traffic. A policeman spotted him and pulled him over. "Hey," the officer asked, "just where do you think you're going?"

"I don't know," the drunk answered, "but it looks like I'm late because everybody's coming back." The same thing happens to us. We get caught up in the crowd and in the condition of our lives, and we wind up going the wrong way down a one-way street. We don't know where we're going, but because everybody else seems to be *coming* from there, we keep heading in that direction.

Our identities come from our position in Christ. That's where there's power to change, power over death, and power to live the radical Christian life. As we identify with Christ, and accept and act on our position in Him, we know who we are and what we're all about. Then when we get our act together, we won't forget where we put it. It will be in Christ.

FIVE
LIVING ON
A HIGH SALARY

While reading the paper recently, I came across an article about an unusual robbery. It seems that a man walked into a business, pointed a gun at the first person he saw, and said, "I want to see the paymaster. Who writes the checks around here?"

After a few seconds of silence a little guy in the back raised his hand and squeaked, "I do."

"All right," the robber said. "Hand over the money!"

"What money do you want me to hand over?" asked the paymaster timidly.

"I don't want the salaries," the robber said. "Pay these people their wages. Just give me their withholding taxes, pension funds, group insurance premiums, hospitalization payments, disability, and welfare!"

Then there was the lady who received a raise from her boss. She was told, "Now, I don't want you to say anything to anyone about the salary I'm paying you."

"Don't worry," she said, "I'm just as ashamed of it as you are."

Everyone is concerned about salary. What we make never

54

seems to be enough to make ends meet, especially after everything is taken out, so we're always on the lookout for jobs that pay more. We're not looking for more *work*, which is supposedly the basis of what we're paid; we just want jobs with higher salaries.

God is concerned about salary too. But in His economy, the payment system is different. It's not like the one at work where we get paid the same no matter what we do or don't do. With God we get paid on the basis of what we do and don't do: "For we must all appear before the Judgment Seat of Christ, that each one may be recompensed for his deeds in the body, according to what he has done, whether good or bad" (2 Cor. 5:10).

Romans 6:23 reveals the pay scale: "For the wages of sin is death, but the free gift of God is eternal life in Christ Jesus our Lord." The salary for sin is death, separation from God, and separation from people. But when we come into a relationship with God through Christ, we receive the free gift of eternal life. Both are high salaries; it's just a matter of which one we'll receive—death or life.

THE OLD MAN

God's payment system is explained in Romans 6:3-14 in terms of the flesh, the spirit, and the will. Before you become a believer, your will is completely enslaved by the flesh. It's the principle discussed in chapter 4 of this book; the flesh, the old sin nature, is the master and you are its slave.

The way you get out of being a slave is to die. When you're dead, the flesh can no longer be master over you. It doesn't control you anymore.

THE NEW MAN

When you come into a relationship with God, when you accept Jesus Christ as your personal Saviour, God basically does three things. First, He makes you dead to sin so you are no longer a slave to your old sin nature; second, He unites you with Christ's resurrection and makes you alive to God; and third, He puts the Holy Spirit inside your spirit. Your spirit is the immaterial part of you, and everyone has one whether he's a believer or nonbeliever.

When God unites you with Christ's resurrection and makes you alive to Him, your spirit comes to life. Hence the term "born again"; what is born again is your spirit. "That which is born of the [Holy] Spirit is spirit" (John 3:6, brackets added). Up until that point, your spirit is dead toward God, you are separated from Him, and without His power will face eternal death.

When you receive Christ, God also creates a whole new you. "If any man is in Christ, he is a new creature" (2 Cor. 5:17). Instead of your old sin nature that was dead to God, you have a whole new nature that is alive toward God.

It's easy to take for granted what God has done for you and start looking for Him to do something else. But don't forget that He has freed you from the slavery of your old sin nature and given you a certificate of release so that you can be His child and live life for Him. Not only that, but He has given you a new nature, a whole newborn spirit living inside you with new desires and energy. You now have the old sin nature in the flesh, the new nature in your newborn spirit, and God living inside you with His Holy Spirit. God has performed spiritual surgery on your life!

THE TWO MEN

Or do you not know that all of us who have been baptized into Christ Jesus have been baptized into His death? Therefore we have been buried with Him through baptism into death, in order that as Christ was raised from the dead through the glory of the Father, so we too might walk in newness of life. For if we have become united with Him in the likeness of His death, certainly we shall be also in the likeness of His resurrection, knowing this, that our old self was crucified with Him, that our body of sin might be done away with, that we should no longer be slaves to sin; for he who has died is freed from sin (Rom. 6:3-7).

There's some confusion as to who is the "old self," the old man, in this passage. The old man is not the flesh; it is the will connected to the flesh (see figure 3). It's the old manner of life. When you come into a relationship with God through Jesus Christ your old man is crucified, put to death, freeing you to put off your old manner of life and put on your new one. But just because you are no longer enslaved to your sin nature doesn't mean it no longer exists. As long as our flesh is with us, the sin nature will be there, pulling us toward sin and away from God. God's spiritual operation in our lives simply makes it possible for us to put off the old man and put on the new one. We now have the choice to no longer serve sin.

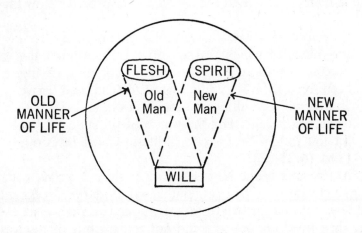

FIGURE 3

What then? Shall we sin because we are not under law but under grace? May it never be! Do you know that when you present yourselves to someone as slaves for obedience, you are slaves of the one whom you obey, either of sin resulting in death, or of obedience resulting in righteousness? But thanks be to God that though you were slaves of sin, you became obedient from the heart to that form of teaching to which you were committed, and having been freed from sin, you became slaves of righteousness. I am speaking in human terms because of the weakness of your flesh. For just as you presented your members as slaves to impurity and to lawlessness, resulting in further lawlessness, so now present your members as slaves to righteousness, resulting in sanctification. For when you were slaves of sin, you were free in regard to righteousness (6:15-20).

When we were slaves to sin, we didn't know what was right and wrong. We were "free in regard to righteousness." As believers, we *do* know what is right and wrong. That's why people sometimes have more struggles as believers than they had as nonbelievers. Before they didn't know better; now they do.

Therefore what benefit were you then deriving from the things of which you are now ashamed? For the outcome of those things is death. But now having been freed from sin and enslaved to God, you derive your benefit, resulting in sanctification, and the outcome, eternal life. For the wages of sin is death, but the free gift of God is eternal life in Christ Jesus our Lord (6:21-23).

At the time of the New Testatment writers, a slave could be freed by death or by being purchased. Both the Greeks and the Jews allowed their slaves to save money over the years and buy their freedom, but they did not actually buy themselves. They put the money in the temple treasury, and when there was enough the master and the slave would go to the temple. There the master would receive the money for the purchase of his slave, and the slave would be given a certificate of freedom.

At that point the slave gained both freedom and responsibility. He could never be obligated to the former master again, but he had to be active in temple life.

That's the image Paul is using in Romans 6. Once we come into a relationship with God we are free—we have our certificate and can serve God. We are no longer enslaved by the old master of sin; we can put off the old man and put on the new man. God wants us to know that, to count on it, and to act on our freedom, to stop doing what we used to do and start doing what we ought to do.

God's payment system involves a high salary. We can remain in the old man and collect our "pay" by dying for an eternity. Or we can accept the free gift of eternal life in Christ and put on the new man. It's up to us.

SIX
SUPERNATURAL
CHRISTIANITY
NATURALLY

od, through the work of His Son, has enabled us to put off the old man and put on the new man. He wants us to really believe that, count on it, and act like it. Because Christ has purchased our freedom, we are no longer obligated to our old manner of life; instead we are obligated to the new.

The new man is able to put on a new way of life—but how does that translate into behavior? Christians have been asking that question since day one, and they keep coming up with some of the same insane answers. I speak against their insanity whenever I can, and so does Paul in Romans 6. The insane answers are heresy—a doctrinal departure from revealed truth—which came from a group called the Gnostics.

The Gnostics were spiritual "head trippers." They believed that God's spiritual energy and power were contained in the word *Christ,* and that they had the secret to releasing it. Through acquiring more knowledge, they felt, they could obtain more energy and power from God.

Paul says that's not what Christ is all about; that's not how you get the energy and power of God. Christ is not just a spirit or a form of energy or a flow of power. He is not just a force that blesses us if we do this and doesn't bless us if we do that. He doesn't perform according to our demands, and He doesn't play games.

Christ is a person. He is the Son of God who died on the cross so we might also die and be freed, who rose from the dead so we might also be raised, who gave His life for us. All He asks—now that He has purchased us and we are His slaves—is that we not be obligated to our old manner of life. Instead we are to be obligated to our new manner of life.

Two Extremes

There are two philosophical extremes in our world. Those at one extreme say everything operates according to natural laws, that events flow naturally without God. Things function as they always have. Cause and effect are the same today as they were at the beginning of time, and they'll continue to be the same in the future. This extreme is atheistic naturalism.

The other extreme is superstitious supernaturalism. At this end of the spectrum people go down deep and stay down long and never come up for air, philosophically speaking. Superstitious supernaturalism is basically the Gnostic heresy, in which more knowledge is stashed and stored and some secret is revealed and some energy and power released. This extreme has infiltrated Christianity since the beginning, and it always has been and still is absolutely wrong.

Lots of people have filled their heads with knowledge, but they have never done anything about it. The content of their minds changes, but their manner of life doesn't. Radical Christianity is not atheistic naturalism, nor is it superstitious supernaturalism. Radical Christianity means focusing on God's *supernatural* work in your life and then following up with your *natural* response to Him.

SUPERSTITIOUS CHRISTIANITY

Superstition comes in various forms, but it always ends up focusing on something other than the truly supernatural. For example, I often hear people say, "I want to be able to touch God and to have Him touch me." They feel that occurs in various ways, for example during a certain service when the music is "just right" and a specific song is sung. Then, they say, God touches them.

I have a real hard time believing that! The people involved may have had a warm feeling or may have been moved by a song—that happens to me with a couple of songs that were sung at my parents' funerals—but I don't believe anyone "touches" God at that point.

People are looking for all kinds of miraculous things to happen in their lives. They're looking for ecstatic experiences in which they can receive some special gift. They're looking for situations in which they can commune with God. What these situations must be like depends on the people. For some they must include organ music; for others, stained glass; for others, communion. Then God will "be there" and "bless them."

Others are looking for "something more." They stumble over what God has already done in their lives and what He asks them to do, and they look for more.

Some people, for instance, believe you have to "pray more." If you pray more and in a certain way, they say, then God will do unusual things in your life. The Bible never says to pray *more*. It says we should be people of prayer, and that when a righteous man prays effectively it can accomplish much (James 5:16). Christ had some strong things to say about the professional pray-ers of His day, those who stood on street corners and repeated elaborate words from empty hearts. He said prayer is talking with God, and when you know who you are and what He has done in your heart, you can communicate with Him.

Other people believe you have to *study more*, and they're

always looking for those who can show them how to *really* study, to get down to the "deeper" things. They think if they could only understand the Greek or Hebrew they would be able to get close to God. I've studied both languages, and I can guarantee they don't get you any closer to God. Of course, the work of trying to *learn* them might drive you to pray more!

Then there are people who look for God to lead them in a supernatural way. They are willing to copy anyone they think God might be leading.

Sometimes I wind up in places I don't usually go, with people I don't know, and while there I'm often able to help people trust the Lord or let Him take control of their lives. I think it happens when I'm more open and listening to what's going on around me. I believe God does more or less the same thing with all of us when we're willing to be used where we are.

Once, for example, I went into a restaurant just to get away for an hour and do some work. It was only the second time I had ever been there. I sat in the corner, ordered some iced tea, and pulled out my papers. When the waiter brought my tea he said, "Hey, man, what are you doing?"

"Well," I said, "I'm working on a message. I'm a speaker."

"Where do you speak?" he asked.

"Actually, I speak all over the world," I answered, and I gave him the itinerary for my next trip.

"That's incredible!" he said.

"I also speak every Sunday," I added.

"Are you a minister?" he asked.

I hesitated, then said yes.

"Wow," came his response. It turned out that the guy was a Christian who was ready to call it quits and end his life. And there I was—the only customer in the place. And he was the only waiter.

How did that happen? Why did I wind up at that restaurant when that particular waiter was working? We ask those kinds of questions because we think that if we could get the answers we could reproduce the situation. If I told you exactly how I felt that day and what was going through my mind, you could go out and try to feel and think the same way and see whether God would lead you to a restaurant where there was someone who was considering suicide. But God doesn't lead His people in masses by giving them "something more." He leads them individually as they relate to Him.

God leads us through our desires as long as we keep in touch with Him, talk with Him, and respond to what He's doing in our hearts. God has freed us from death to live life, and He wants us to spread that around wherever we go. I'm convinced that at times God has me in certain places to meet certain people, but I'm also convinced that God doesn't want me to put a patent on those times and sell them to you so you can try to reproduce my experiences. God will lead you just as He leads me, but we must be looking for His leading and not "something more."

Looking for "something more" is part of the Gnostic heresy. It's putting more stuff in my head so that I wind up focusing on something else—something superstitious—rather than on the truly supernatural.

SMOTS AND BLIND LEAPS

It's absolutely insane the way some people try to live the Christian life. Because of their insanity they wind up doing a little bit of everything except ministering to people. We love our SMOTS—Secret Meetings of the Saints—in which we keep the same group of people together. We might let a few new people in, but only if God knocks on the door or it's next to impossible to get out of witnessing to them. We like our SMOTS meetings because they're comfortable. We don't have to move or meet new people, much less meet any needs they might have.

SMOTS meetings never occurred in the Bible. In fact,

Scripture doesn't contain an *inkling* of anything *like* them. The early Christians were too busy ministering to people—meeting them, caring for their needs, and sharing the Good News. Christians have all of eternity to go to SMOTS meetings, to gather a few people together and sit and soak and share. They have only a few short years to minister.

While some people are praying more, studying more, looking for God to lead them, and attending SMOTS, others are making blind leaps. They're putting their faith in the dark without rhyme or reason, claiming this person and that thing. The Bible doesn't teach that. You never find people in the Bible claiming and believing things God didn't say He would do.

That's why Paul says so strongly and repeatedly, in effect, "I want you to know some things. I want you to know that you are now free to live. You have a newborn spirit and the Holy Spirit inside of you. I want you to count on that, and I want you to act like a freed slave—like God's slave. Your only two obligations are not to be obligated to the old master, and instead to be obligated to God."

SUPERNATURAL WORK, NATURAL RESPONSE

Radical Christianity focuses on what is truly *supernatural*, not on what is *superstitious*. It focuses on the supernatural work of God in your life, and then it asks you to follow up on His work with your natural response. I call it "supernatural Christianity naturally."

God will work in your life; He will motivate you, guide you, and use you, but you must be involved. This message is found all the way through Scripture: God's work demands your response.

Stop looking at the outward things, the "we should do this" and "we shouldn't do that," and look at what's happened inside your own life. God has performed a supernatural operation there! Don't shrug it off and try to figure out how to get something miraculous to happen. Something miraculous has *already* happened! God has already done His work, and He promises to keep doing it right up until the end. All He wants you to do is to respond to it.

When—and usually *only* when—we respond to God, our lives begin to be transformed. We start to change. Maybe there are some things in your life that need changing, and you're willing and vulnerable enough to say, "God, I want You to change these things in my life." For example, you may be known for telling dirty jokes, for passing porno around the office, or for being the life of the party when you're drunk. Maybe you're known for the way you cheat on business deals—or on your mate. Maybe you're known for how tough and rough and gruff you are in relationships. Whatever it is, you're known for something and you know you need to change. There is hope for change, but not until you focus on God's supernatural work in your life. You have to know you're free, count on it, and then you can act like it.

If you don't focus on God's supernatural work in your life, you wind up *reforming* instead of *transforming*. You end up redoing and reshaping and repatching, but not changing. Only the power of God can produce change. To continue playing with superstitious Christianity and looking for "something else" and "something more" is insanity. You have been freed to live the Christian life; now *do* it. Focus on what God has done for you and enjoy it!

This idea first began to sink in for me after I graduated from seminary. I knew what my professors had taught me, but once I got my degree, I determined I didn't *really* know anything! I got down on my knees and into the Word daily, trying to find God. I kept saying, "God, if You're there I've got to know it." The problem was that I was looking for Him "out there." I was looking for some experience to let me know He was there, even though He'd already proven His presence by working in my life.

I read and reread Romans 6. Finally I realized God was

there. I could know that; all I had to do was *act* like it. Anything short of that was insanity.

The following story illustrates the point. A policeman was driving down a long desert road when he spotted three men walking across the sand. As he got closer to them he realized each man was carrying something strange. One man had a washtub full of water on his back, the second man was carrying a large combination safe, and the third man had a car door on his back.

The highway patrolman couldn't believe it. He stopped right in front of them and said, "Hold it, you guys. What in the world are you doing with these strange things on your backs?"

The guy with the washtub spoke up first. "Well, I'm carrying this tub full of water and this washcloth so I can dip the washcloth in the tub and wipe my face when I get hot."

"OK," said the policeman. "What about you?" he asked, pointing to the second guy.

"I'm carrying this safe so when I get hot I can unlock it, get some money out, and give it to the guy with the tub. Then he gets his cloth out and wipes my face."

The policeman shook his head in disbelief, but figured he may as well let the third guy explain about the car door.

"Well," said the third man, "when it gets hot I roll the window down and it seems to cool me off a little bit."

Practicing superstitious Christianity is just as insane as carrying a door through the desert and rolling the window down when you want to cool off. We've been freed to live. We don't have to look for something miraculous to happen in our lives—we have the miracle of Christ. We need to focus on God's supernatural work in our lives and then follow up with our natural response to Him. It's supernatural Christianity—naturally.

SEVEN
NORMAL CHRISTIAN LIVING

So far our study of Romans has been primarily theological. We've explored man's predicament, the fact that he is alienated from God (1:18–3:20); his new past, created when he accepts Christ's payment for his sins and is declared righteous (3:21–5:21); and his new position, being dead to sin and alive to God (6). Romans 7 and 8 deal with man's new power, and in these two critical chapters Paul moves from the theological to the practical.

We have heard the Judge's demand, "You must pay for your sin." We have seen Him step down from the bench and pay the penalty Himself, and we have accepted His payment. Now we must answer this question: "How do we live the Christian life?"

THE STRUGGLE

Chapter 7 begins by reiterating our new position of being dead to sin and alive to God (7:1-6). Paul uses the illustration of remarriage after the death of a partner; when one partner dies, the other is released from the old bond of marriage and freed to marry again. The same happens when we die to the old "marriage bond" of sin. We are freed to be joined in a new marriage bond with God.

Then Paul asks a question about the Law: "Is the Law sin?" (7:7) Is this Law that's causing me so much difficulty an evil thing? "May it never be!" he answers in the same verse. The Law is God's standard that tells us what we're to do and how we're to do it. It isn't sin. It simply shows us where we fall short. "On the contrary, I would not have come to know sin except through the Law; for I would not have known about coveting if the Law had not said, 'You shall not covet' " (7:7). That's what the Law is all about. It's a tutor to teach us and a mirror to remind us that we fall short—that we can't make it on our own.

As Paul moves from judicial freedom to experiential freedom, from the theological to the practical, a struggle emerges. The same thing happens to us as we try to live the Christian life:

For that which I am doing, I do not understand; for I am not practicing what I would like to do, but I am doing the very thing I hate. But if I do the very thing I do not wish to do, I agree with the Law, confessing that it is good. So now, no longer am I the one doing it, but sin which indwells me. For I know that nothing good dwells in me, that is, in my flesh; for the wishing is present in me, but the doing of the good is not. For the good that I wish, I do not do; but I practice the very evil that I do not wish. But if I am doing the very thing I do not wish, I am no longer the one doing it, but sin which dwells in me. I find then the principle that evil is present in me, the one who wishes to do good (7:15-21).

Our struggle stems from the principle of evil, from the sin that dwells in us. We honestly want to do good, and we try to do good, but instead we do bad. We wind up doing what we don't want to do, and we don't do what we want to do. At first Paul's words sound like double-talk, but as we sort out his struggle we can all identify with him.

THE REASON FOR THE STRUGGLE

We know God's standard is right: "For I joyfully concur with the Law of God in the inner man" (7:22). We genuinely desire to live up to that standard, but the principle of evil keeps pulling us away from God. There is "a different law in the members of my body, waging war against the law of my mind, and making me a prisoner of the law of sin which is in my members" (7:23). Romans 6 assures us we're dead to sin and alive to God, but we still have the old sin nature inside us. Like a giant magnet, it continues to pull us away from God.

The flesh/sin nature principle wages war against the spirit/new nature principle. Paul says it this way in Galatians: "For the flesh sets its desire against the Spirit, and the Spirit against the flesh; for these are in opposition to one another, so that you may not do the things that you please" (Gal. 5:17). Despite the capital "S," I believe the spirit spoken of in this verse is not the Holy Spirit. It's your newborn spirit, your new nature which the Holy Spirit has created. That's what the sin nature wages war against.

THE REALITY OF THE STRUGGLE

The heart of Romans 7 is in the last two verses: "Wretched man that I am! Who will set me free from the body of this death? Thanks be to God through Jesus Christ our Lord! So then, on the one hand I myself with my mind am serving the Law of God, but on the other, with my flesh the law of sin" (7:24-25).

When Paul says, "Wretched man that I am!" he does not mean, "Sinful man that I am!" The word *wretched* means miserable—pressured, distressed, torn. It literally means to be constantly knocked around and pulled in different directions.

Paul is a wretched man not because he is a sinner, but because he cannot do what he wants to do. He is miserable because the two principles are warring inside him.

The Living Bible ends chapter seven in the middle of verse 25: "Thank God! It has been done by Jesus Christ our Lord. He has set me free" (7:25, TLB). That's wonderful, but that's not where the chapter ends. It continues: "So then, on the one hand I myself with my mind am serving the Law of God, but on the other, with my flesh the law of sin" (7:25). In effect, Paul ends chapter seven with, "I am miserable. I am torn between two principles. I don't do what I want to do, and I wind up doing what I don't want to do."

Paul is speaking only about himself, isn't he? Surely he doesn't mean this applies to all believers! He must be talking just about believers who aren't really committed, or those who haven't really received "the gifts." No! He's talking about *every* believer, about the normal experience of the Christian life. He's giving us this picture of reality so we can learn to deal with the struggle more successfully.

Most of us don't like what Paul has to say here because we don't want to admit there will always be a struggle. We want to be delivered completely, forever, to never have to struggle again. There is a way to avoid the struggle permanently, but it's terminal, because the only escape from this miserable situation is death. As long as we're alive, the struggle's on. We want to do right, but we don't. And we feel horrible about it.

THE RESISTANCE TO THE STRUGGLE

Though the only way to get rid of the struggle permanently is to die, man in his desperation has found a couple of ways that work temporarily. One way is to reduce God's standards. "Surely God didn't mean it when He wrote those things down in the Bible," man says. "God probably just ran out of things to do and thought we might have fun playing around with His Book, as if it were a giant game of monopoly or something. And besides, what would preachers preach on if they didn't have the Bible? Sunday mornings wouldn't be the same. God's standards aren't to be taken seriously. Why, a loving God wouldn't say those things."

The other way to temporarily get rid of the struggle is to claim that man is equal with God. That's what the Gnostics did. They said, "If you find the secret you can touch God." People are still saying that. Richard Bach's *Jonathan Livingston Seagull,* a bestselling novel in the early 1970s, tells the story of a seagull who wanted to fly at 350 miles per hour. Such a jet-propelled bird doesn't exist, but somehow Jonathan thought he could soar above the others at that speed. He had the urge to be free, to escape everything, to not have to struggle anymore.

A lot of the cults are doing the same thing. They're raising the level of man so their members don't have to struggle any more. "You too can be like Jesus Christ," they say. "You too can be like God. As a matter of fact, you can *be* God." Some Christians practically say the same thing: "If you only had the secret, you could touch God. Lucky for you, I've got it, and I'll make you a great deal."

Whether it's reducing God's standards or raising man to be equal with God, any attempt to get rid of the struggle is wrong and it won't work. As long as we are alive, the flesh and the spirit will war within us. With one pulling us away from God and one pulling us toward God, we will constantly struggle to do what we want and avoid what we don't want. It is the misery we cannot escape, the struggle we all face, the unavoidable experience of every believer.

In other words, it is normal Christian living.

EIGHT
A SHOT
OF SPIRITUAL
ADRENALINE

*I*n his effort to show practically how we can live the Christian life, Paul in chapter 7 presents the struggle every believer faces. He asks, "How are we going to get out of this mess? How are we going to get out of this wretched, miserable condition we're in?" Romans 7 is definitely the "bad news" side of the story, but Romans 8 breaks through with an answer and some "good news." I call this good news "spiritual adrenaline," and when we're injected with it, our miserable lives turn into meaningful ones.

In chapter 8 Paul brings the dilemma of chapter 7 right down to the here and now. I strongly believe that if Christianity won't work in the here and now, it won't work anywhere. That's why I'm willing to risk throwing it out to you and saying, "Try it!"

WHERE THINGS ALWAYS GO RIGHT
The problem is that a lot of people think that when Christianity works, everything works out right. That's a bunch of bunk! That kind of thinking may make the Christian life seem

more exciting, but all it really does is dig an escape tunnel. "Well, I thought this would all work out because God takes care of His children," we may say indignantly when things go wrong. God *does* take care of His children, but that doesn't mean everything works out to our liking.

Not until you get to heaven will everything in your life work out right. So if smooth sailing is what you're asking for, the only way God can grant your request is to have you join Him in the hereafter!

I mentioned that to a woman I was counseling one day. She had been starting her sentences with phrases like, "I thought God would . . . God was supposed to . . . I prayed and God didn't do. . . ."

Finally I stopped her. "Do you know what you're asking for?" I said.

"No," she answered.

"You're asking to die!"

"*Die?*" she shrieked. "I've never even *thought* about killing myself!"

"Maybe not, but you are asking God to take you early."

"How am I doing that?" she asked.

"By asking Him to make everything perfect," I said. "The only place everything is perfect is in heaven!"

The song that says, "This is my Father's world" isn't telling the whole truth. This is *not* God's world now. It belongs to Satan, and he is the god of this world. If this were God's world we wouldn't be in this miserable condition, and we wouldn't need the four shots of adrenaline Paul gives us in Romans 8.

UNCONDEMNED LIFE

I *love* this first shot: "There is therefore now no condemnation for those who are in Christ Jesus" (Rom. 8:1).

Psychologists and counselors have been talking a lot about "shoulds" lately. That's because a lot of people have fallen prey to the tyranny of "shoulds" and have become shackled by them. These shoulds are contemporary ones: "You should have this; you should do that. . . ." I hate the shoulds, especially when they're condemning ones. No one deserves or needs our shoulds. "There is therefore now no condemnation [no condemning shoulds] for those who are in Christ Jesus" [brackets added].

However, that doesn't mean it's wise to do anything you want. Paul also writes, "All things are lawful for me, but not all things are profitable" (1 Cor. 6:12). Everything is lawful, but not everything is expedient. Just because something is lawful doesn't make it helpful! I've been saying that for years. You can do this and you can do that. If you do this you'll get bruised, and if you do that you'll get blessed. You can take it or leave it.

When we're involved in the struggle of this world—when our old nature is trying to trip us up and tempt us and pull us away from God—we can end up under a pile. It's messy and discouraging, and when we're under this pile we need some spiritual adrenaline. Our first shot is an uncondemned life—a life no longer run by shoulds:

> For the law of the Spirit of life in Christ Jesus has set you free from the law of sin and of death. For what the Law could not do, weak as it was through the flesh, God did: sending His own Son in the likeness of sinful flesh and as an offering for sin, He condemned sin in the flesh, in order that the requirement of the Law might be fulfilled in us, who do not walk according to the flesh, but according to the Spirit [our newborn spirit] (Rom. 8:2-4, brackets added).

As previously mentioned, when the word *spirit* is used the subject is not always the Holy Spirit. In Romans 8:5-11 the meaning of the word shuttles between "Holy Spirit" and "our newborn spirit." It's the same word, but the context and lack of the Greek article translated *the* tells us which spirit is referred to:

For those who are according to the flesh set their minds on the things of the flesh, but those who are according to the [newborn] Spirit, the things of the [Holy] Spirit. For the mind set on the flesh is death, but the mind set on the [Holy] Spirit is life and peace, because the mind set on the flesh is hostile toward God; for it does not subject itself to the Law of God, for it is not even able to do so; and those who are in the flesh cannot please God. (8:5-8)

However you are not in the flesh but in the [newborn] Spirit, if indeed the [Holy] Spirit of God dwells in you. But if anyone does not have the [Holy] Spirit of Christ, he does not belong to Him. And if Christ is in you, though the body is dead because of sin, yet the [newborn] spirit is alive because of righteousness. But if the [Holy] Spirit of Him who raised Jesus from the dead dwells in you, He who raised Christ Jesus from the dead will also give life to your mortal bodies through His [Holy] Spirit who indwells you (8:9-11, brackets added).

I have added the brackets in these verses because of the interplay of the two spirits and the confusion that results when the two are not differentiated. When we come into a relationship with God through Christ, the Holy Spirit creates in us a newborn spirit, one which wants to please God. The Holy Spirit comes to live in that newborn spirit. He indwells us, resides in us, and gives us spiritual adrenaline when we need it.

There have been times, for example, when I've gotten up to speak but didn't feel like it or didn't have anything to say. Invariably, after I have mumbled away, someone will come up to me and say, "Wow, that was the most wonderful message I've ever heard!" *What*? I think. *Surely I must be hearing things! How could that person have possibly heard something wonderful?*

It's not that I take speaking lightly. When I speak I give it everything I've got. I work long, hard hours to be interesting, stimulating, and motivating, but my *speaking* doesn't change people's lives. I make my preparations, keep people awake for about thirty minutes, plant some truth in their minds, and then God takes their lives and works them over. When I don't deliver the goods so swiftly, God just shoots more "adrenaline" into the deal. When I know what I should be saying and I'm getting it said, He can cut down the dosage.

The Holy Spirit, living in our newborn spirits, gives us a shot of the uncondemned life. When we're torn, He wants us to realize that because He lives inside us we are free from condemnation. No one can condemn us anymore. God isn't going to condemn us, so neither can anyone else.

GRADUATION

So then, brethren, we are under obligation, not to the flesh, to live according to the flesh—for if you are living according to the flesh, you must die; but if by the [newborn] Spirit you are putting to death the deeds of the body, you will live. For all who are being led by the [Holy] Spirit of God, these are sons of God. For you have not received a spirit of slavery leading to fear again, but you have received a [newborn] spirit of adoption as sons by which we cry out, "Abba! Father!" The [Holy] Spirit Himself bears witness with our [newborn] spirit that we are children of God, and if children, heirs also, heirs of God and fellow-heirs with Christ, if indeed we suffer with Him in order that we may also be glorified with Him (8:12-17, brackets added).

The second shot of adrenaline is our graduation. Notice verse 14: "For all who are being led by the [Holy] Spirit of God, these are sons of God." God assures us that He will continue to lead us toward righteousness, toward a day He calls adoption. He doesn't give us "a spirit of slavery leading to fear again," but "a spirit of adoption as sons" (8:15). Our adoption takes place when we are given a new body and are finally complete in Him. We are complete in Christ right now, but someday we will stand complete before God, and then our adoption will be final.

The word could really be "graduation." God is going to make us complete, and we are going to graduate. The Holy Spirit is leading us, all the sons of God, toward that graduation. We can count on it.

"The [Holy] Spirit Himself bears witness with our [newborn] spirit that we are children of God" (8:16, brackets added). That's because He's taking us to that graduation. Through the muck and the mire, in spite of the detours we take and the times we get lost, the Spirit leads us back to God. It's one of the greatest promises I know in the Scripture, that when I mess up, the Holy Spirit turns me back toward God. It's another shot of adrenaline!

GLORY

"For I consider that the sufferings of this present time are not worthy to be compared with the glory that is to be revealed to us. For the anxious longing of the creation waits eagerly for the revealing of the sons of God" (8:18-19). Even the creation is waiting for us to graduate, for Christians to be glorified. I've heard lots of preachers say that God will not share His glory with anyone, but that's not true. God is going to share His glory with His children. God is going to glorify us! That's the third shot of adrenaline.

"And not only this, but also we ourselves, having the firstfruits of the Spirit" (8:23). The Greek word translated "firstfruits" is the word *aparche,* which means "beginning." It's related to the word *arrabon* in Ephesians 1:14, which is translated "pledge" or "earnest money," or in the modern Greek, "engagement ring." Both these references are talking about what we have been given in the Holy Spirit. In Him we are given a newborn spirit and the promise—an engagement ring—that He will complete His work in our lives. The Spirit has been given to us as a down payment. Right now we're still in escrow, but the deal will be closed when we graduate and are glorified.

"For in hope we have been saved, but hope that is seen is not hope; for why does one also hope for what he sees? But if we hope for what we do not see, with perseverance we wait eagerly for it. And in the same way the Spirit also helps our weakness" (Rom. 8:24-26). Our weakness is our sin nature. It's what causes us to feel wretched and miserable as our flesh wrestles with our spirit and we struggle not to do what we don't want to do. The only way we can win over our weakness is with a shot of spiritual adrenaline.

"In the same way the Spirit also helps our weakness; for we do not know how to pray as we should, but the Spirit Himself intercedes for us with groanings too deep for words; and He who searches the hearts knows what the mind of the Spirit is, because He intercedes for the saints according to the will of God" (8:26-27). How many times have you not felt like praying, primarily because you didn't know what to say? I've been there many times! Paul says the Holy Spirit helps us win over this too. We need only bow before God and say, "God, things are so messed up I have no idea what to do. I'm just coming to you." The Holy Spirit then takes our weakness, our silence, and translates it to God. He can do that because of this shot of adrenaline, this shot of glory. He wants to glorify us, to lead us to life.

"And we know that God causes all things to work together [with something else] for good to those who love God, to those who are called according to His purpose" (8:28, brackets added). Every time there's a crisis—every time you're under a "pile" and the walls have tumbled down and the roof has caved in and the bottom has fallen out—if you're a believer, God is going to work all things, even the bad ones, together with something else for your good. "For whom He foreknew, He also predestined to become conformed to the image of His Son, that He might be the first-born among many brethren; and whom He predestined, these He also called; and whom He called, these He also justified; and whom He justified, these He also glorified" (8:29-30).

Even when everything is "down and out," God is going to work it together with something else for good. That doesn't mean that what *happened* is good. You don't have to say, "Oh, it's wonderful. I've gone bankrupt and lost my business! Praise the Lord!" The Lord doesn't ask you to be excited about the problems, nor does He promise you'll escape them. He *does* promise to get you through them and to give you meaning—to work them together with something else for good.

UNCONQUERABLE LOVE

What then shall we say to these things? If God is for us, who is against us? He who did not spare His own Son, but delivered Him up for us all, how will He not also with Him freely give us all things? Who will bring a charge against God's elect? God is the One who justifies; who is the one who condemns? Christ Jesus is He who died, yes, rather who was raised, who is at the right hand of God, who also intercedes for us. Who shall separate us from the love of Christ? Shall tribulation, or distress, or persecution, or famine, or nakedness, or peril, or sword? Just as it is written, "For Thy sake we are being put to death all day long; we were considered as sheep to be slaughtered." But in all these things we overwhelmingly conquer through Him who loved us (8:31-37).

"But in all these things," under all these horrible piles of problems, we win—not by a couple of points, not by squeezing through in overtime, but overwhelmingly. We kill them. We absolutely *slaughter* them! Every time it looks like there's no way to shovel ourselves out of a situation, there's a shot of adrenaline, of unconquerable love.

Nothing can separate us from that love, and through it we can conquer anything. "For I am convinced that neither death, nor life, nor angels, nor principalities, nor things present, nor things to come, nor powers, nor height, nor depth, nor any other created thing, shall be able to separate us from the love of God, which is in Christ Jesus our Lord" (8:38-39). Whether it's the things of this world or the more powerful things beyond this world, nothing can separate us from God's love.

This last shot of spiritual adrenaline, unconquerable love, ties in with the first one, an uncondemned life. The greatest need we have is to be loved for who we are. Isn't it great when you know somebody loves and accepts you for who you are? I get tired of being on a treadmill for people, of being the pastor who's supposed to do this and that, of being the Dallas man who should throw in a little Greek here and there. I just want somebody to love me for *me*, mean and raunchy as I am.

God does. He also loves *you* exactly the way *you* are. It's incredible, absolutely incredible. God loves us, and nothing can separate us from His love. What a shot of adrenaline!

"SHOULD" VS. "WANT TO"

The Holy Spirit can turn our wretched, miserable lives into meaningful ones. He can take the tension caused by the struggle between our flesh and our spirit and translate it into the desire and motivation to change. When we accept His shot of spiritual adrenaline, our desires and motivations become life changing, and our lives and lifestyles become meaningful. Instead of being shackled by condemning "shoulds," we are able to do what our newborn spirits want to do. As my uncle used to say, "I do everything I want to now that I'm a Christian, but God has changed my 'want to.'" God can change *your* "want to" if you'll let Him—if you let His Holy Spirit change your misery into a meaningful life.

The trouble is that we get hung up trying to figure out

what's right and what's wrong. We're constantly analyzing and evaluating to determine what "box" something goes in. "Oh, dear," we say. "That activity can't possibly be right. And my, my, that thing must be wrong." We forget that the Holy Spirit says there is no condemnation for those who are in Christ Jesus.

Don't spend your time and energy putting people in boxes. Nobody does everything right—none of us ever has and none of us ever will in this life. We forget that the Holy Spirit's power is inside our bodies, and we focus instead on rigid "shoulds" and "shouldn'ts."

Instead of the letter of the Law, we need the spirit of the Law. Instead of making resolutions and having all kinds of obsessions, we need to be realistic and look for opportunities in Christ. That's why I choose to overlook a lot of things. I believe Christ came with grace and truth—in that order. He didn't beat people up with the truth and then bestow a little grace on them. He overwhelmed them with His grace and then gave them the truth.

This is illustrated by three men on death row who were facing the electric chair. A priest was brought in to speak with them before their fatal moments. He asked the first man, "Would you like to repent of your sin? For if you do, God may spare your life."

"I repent," the man answered. "I need all the help I can get at this point, and I'm willing to do whatever it takes." He got in the chair. They put the headgear on him, strapped him in, pulled the lever, and nothing happened! He was immediately given a pardon and released.

The second man came in. The priest asked him the same question: "Would you like to repent?"

The prisoner had heard what had happened to the first guy. "You betcha!" he blurted out, "I'll take it."

The priest said, "Good. God may spare your life in the same way." The second man got in the chair. They hooked him up, pulled the lever, and again nothing happened. He too was given a full pardon and went on his way.

Finally it was the third man's turn. The priest asked him, "Are you ready to repent? You know if you do God may spare your life and you'll be pardoned. You might walk right out that door and totally turn your life around. You know that God has worked two miracles here today, and you can be the third! What do you think?"

The third guy shrugged his shoulders. "Well, I don't know what I think about that," he said. "But if they'd just hook those two green wires together down there, that thing would work!"

We're a lot like that third guy. We spend so much precious time making sure others are wired together right—that they are eating, drinking, reading, and watching the right stuff and going to the right seminars—that we miss the life God says He came to give us. Christ didn't come to help us escape the problems of life, He came to give life meaning.

We all want our lives to have meaning, but we can't do it without those shots of adrenaline. We can't do it without recognizing how wretched we are—how miserable we are as we're being torn between our old man and our new man, and how much we need the Holy Spirit to change our motivations and desires—our hearts. That's the "bad news" side of the story. The "good news" is that the Holy Spirit offers us four shots of spiritual adrenaline: an uncondemned life, graduation, glory, and unconquerable love. The best news of all is that if we accept His gift our lives will be changed from miserable to meaningful.

NINE
WHEN GOD
BECOMES *A* GOD

A man called a doctor. "Doctor," he pleaded, "could you please get over here immediately? My wife is in terrible pain."

The doctor came right away. "You stay out here," he told the man, "and I'll go in the bedroom and see what's wrong with your wife." The doctor went into the bedroom and shut the door. A few seconds later the man heard his wife screaming. The doctor came out and said, "Excuse me, but do you happen to have a pair of pliers around?"

"Yeah, I do," the man answered. He got the pliers and gave them to the doctor. The doctor went back into the bedroom and the wife's screaming got louder. The poor husband didn't know what was happening. He just sat there wiping his brow and wringing his hands.

Pretty soon the doctor came back out. With an exasperated expression he said, "How about a saw? Do you have a saw?"

The man gulped. "Y-yes," he said." "Just a minute." He got the saw, gave it to the doctor, and the doctor went back into the bedroom. The wife's screaming was becoming unbearable. She sounded like she was being tortured.

The door opened and out came the doctor again, "Look," he said, "I'm really sorry, but I need one more thing. Do you have a hammer and chisel?"

The man couldn't take it anymore. "Hold it!" he said. "What's going on in there? What are you doing to my wife?"

"Your *wife*?" said the doctor. "I haven't even *gotten* to your wife. I can't get my medical bag open!"

I find a lot of people are playing the part of the husband—counting on so-called problem-solvers who can't get their acts together. Others are like the wife—in a lot of pain, waiting for someone to help them. Still others prefer the role of the doctor—trying to help, but unable to get their "medical bags" open. Husband, wife, or doctor, they're all in pretty bad shape.

Everyone is in pretty bad shape. In Romans Paul describes man's pitiful condition—how he is separated from God. Yet God bridges the gap by sending His Son, giving man a new past, a new position, and a new power to live life. This salvation, this healing and wholeness, is for "everyone who believes, to the Jew first and also to the Greek" (Rom. 1:16).

"To the Jew first. . . ." If this salvation is for everyone, why does Romans say, "to the Jew first"? Paul answers that question in Romans 9–11.

Even though Paul was the apostle to the Gentiles, he didn't put the Jews on the sideline. He knew they were God's chosen people and that they had priority. He also knew what God had given the Jewish people: the promises—or covenants between Himself and the nation of Israel; and the prophecies—or predictions of what would happen with those covenants. Thus in Romans 9–11 Paul shows us how the Gospel relates to God's chosen people. I'm going to concentrate on the way of relating that is applicable to everyone, Jew and Gentile.

THE PAST

The nation of Israel has a unique relationship with God and with the Gospel. Paul, a Jew himself, starts chapter 9 with a strong statement about that relationship:

> For I could wish that I myself were accursed, separated from Christ for the sake of my brethren, my kinsmen according to the flesh, who are Israelites, to whom belongs the adoption of sons and the glory and the covenants and the giving of the Law and the temple service and the promises, whose are the fathers, and from whom is the Christ according to the flesh, who is over all, God blessed forever. Amen.
>
> But it is not as though the Word of God has failed. For they are not all Israel who are descended from Israel; neither are they all children because they are Abraham's descendants, but: "Through Isaac your descendants will be named." That is, it is not the children of the flesh who are children of God, but the children of the promise are regarded as descendants (9:3-8).

Those Jewish people who are people of faith and continue to walk with God and believe in Him are the true Israel.

Paul is talking about the past here—about the promises, prophecies, and the Law God gave humankind through the Jewish people. Even Christ the anointed One—the Messiah—came through them. That was all part of God's plan and is consistent with His justice. "What shall we say then? There is no injustice with God, is there? May it never be! For He says to Moses, 'I will have mercy on whom I have mercy, and I will have compassion on whom I have compassion.' So then it does not depend on the man who wills or the man who runs, but on God who has mercy" (9:14-16). God's plan is just and righteous and includes Israel, no matter what the past has been like.

So then He has mercy on whom He desires, and He hardens whom He desires. You will say to me then, "Why does He still find fault? For who resists His will?" On the contrary, who are you, O man, who answers back to God? The thing molded will not say to the molder, "Why did you make me like this," will it? Or does not the potter have a right over the clay, to make from the same lump one vessel for honorable use, and another for common use? (9:18-21)

Later Paul quotes a prophecy from Hosea: "I will call those who are not My people, 'My people.' And her who was not beloved, 'beloved.' And it shall be that in the place where it was said to them, 'You are not My people,' there they shall be called sons of the living God" (9:25-26). This prophecy from the Jewish past says that some who were not God's people before are going to be His people in the future. Those people are the Gentiles, and they can enjoy the same full relationship with God that the Jews had in the past.

THE PRESENT

With the Gentiles in the picture, we come to the Jewish people in the present. "What shall we say then? That Gentiles, who did not pursue righteousness, attained righteousness, even the righteousness which is by faith; but Israel, pursuing a law of righteousness, did not arrive at that law. Why? Because they did not pursue it by faith, but as though it were by works" (9:30-32).

There are two ways of righteousness, two ways of coming into a relationship with God. One is the way of faith and the other is the way of the Law. Most Jews chose the way of the Law, trying to be perfect, and it didn't work. It doesn't work for Gentiles either.

In the past the Jews had the promises of God, the prophecies of God, and the position of being God's primary people. In the present the Jews have been rejected by God—only partially, not permanently—because of their rejection of Him. They have failed to recognize one thing: "For Christ is the end of the Law for righteousness to everyone who believes" (10:4). The Jewish people failed to recognize Christ as the end of the Law.

In this case the word "end" means not the cessation of the Law but the completion of the Law. The Jewish people have been trying to keep the way of the Law rather than keeping the way of faith. They have not been able to see nor have they been willing to believe that Jesus as the Messiah is the completion of the Law, and therefore they've been side-tracked for a while. They may certainly come to the Lord in the present, but they must come by the only way possible— the way of faith. There is no way to get there by the way of the Law.

The way to God is the same in the Old Testament as it is in the New, for Jew and Gentile alike. "For the Scripture says, 'Whoever believes in Him will not be disappointed.' For there is no distinction between Jew and Greek; for the same Lord is Lord of all, abounding in riches for all who call upon Him; for 'Whoever will call upon the name of the Lord will be saved'" (10:11-13).

Speaking of the salvation of the Jewish people, Paul writes, "How then shall they call upon Him in whom they have not believed? And how shall they believe in Him whom they have not heard? And how shall they hear without a preacher? And how shall they preach unless they are sent? Just as it is written, 'How beautiful are the feet of those who bring glad tidings of good things!'" (10:14-15) In order for Jewish people to come to the Lord, someone must tell them about Jesus the Messiah—that He is the end of the Law. Then they can call on the Lord and find salvation—not by the way of the Law, by perfection, because they are special, or because they have the promises and prophecies—but because they are standing before God by faith, having accepted Jesus as the Messiah.

THE FUTURE

Romans 11, the final chapter on the relationship of the Gospel to the Jewish people, concerns their future and the coming restoration. The Jewish people had a relationship with God that was unique, but because they rejected Him, He rejected them. In a sense Israel has been replaced by the church until the promises and prophecies offered to Israel in the past are fulfilled. There are two essential things to remember about Israel's broken relationship with God. First, the present rejection of Israel is not total. Even though many Jewish people have completely rejected God, they have not been completely rejected by Him. Second, the present rejection of the Jewish people by God is not final.

One of the reasons God brought the Gentiles into the picture was to make the Jewish people jealous:

I say then, they did not stumble so as to fall, did they? May it never be! But by their transgression salvation has come to the Gentiles, to make them jealous. Now if their transgression be riches for the world and their failure be riches for the Gentiles, how much more will their fulfillment be! But I am speaking to you who are Gentiles. Inasmuch then as I am an apostle of Gentiles, I magnify my ministry, if somehow I might move to jealousy my fellow countrymen and save some of them (11:11-14).

Paul wanted to make his Jewish brethren jealous by sharing God's salvation with the Gentiles. Even though I'm not Jewish, that's my theme too as I share the Gospel with Jewish people.

INTRODUCING THE MESSIAH

I used to work with a Christian organization at the American University in Washington, D.C., a Methodist school with a seventy percent Jewish population. One day the national officers of a Jewish organization asked me to come speak to them about our work on campus.

It was definitely one of the most exciting experiences of my life. They threatened to kill me and said they were willing to die themselves to get me off campus! I knew the accusations they had made against me were false, but I also knew I wouldn't be able to convince them on my own. "I'll make you a deal," I said to their spokesman. "We've seen 220 students in the past several months. I'll give you all their names, and if you can find one of them that was turned off by us or believes we're anti-Semitic, I'll leave the campus and never come back."

The spokesman was ecstatic! When I got him a copy of the names, he grabbed it and took off, assured of his organization's success and my imminent departure from the university.

Over the next couple weeks the Jewish organization contacted many of the students we had talked to, but I didn't hear from the spokesman or anyone else. Then one day I was walking across campus with a guy from my staff—a big football player I'd asked to be my unofficial body guard after I'd been threatened—and I saw the spokesman. "Hey," I said, "can I talk to you for a minute?"

"Uh—no," he stammered. "I'm busy right now."

"Oh, come on," I said. "I just want to know what you've found out. Have you talked to anyone who thinks we're anti-Semitic yet?"

He hesitated. "No, not yet."

"OK," I said. "Let me know when you do." He never did let me know, and I knew why. We were running around making the Jewish students jealous. In fact, they even liked us, because we were more Jewish than they were.

Often these students would ask me, "Are you a Christian?"

"Well," I'd reply, "that's an offensive term to you, isn't it? Actually, I prefer to call myself a Messi-Jew."

"Huh? What's a 'messy-Jew'?"

"A *Messi-anic* Jew," I'd say. "Though I must confess I'm

not really Jewish. But I'd like to be, and I'm involved in a movement called 'Messianic Judaism.' "

"Really?"

"Yeah. We believe the Messiah has already come, and we know who He is."

"How do you know that, and who is He?"

"Well, I'd be glad to go through the Old Testament with you and search it out together." It would take a long time before my coworkers and I got around to saying the Messiah was Jesus. In fact, we never actually had to say it. We would just keep moving through the Old Testament, and the Jewish students would come to that conclusion on their own.

Most Gentiles don't even know what's in the Old Testament, much less believe it. But lots of Jewish people know God's past promises and prophecies. If I were to tell the Gentiles that the Messiah was supposed to be born in Bethlehem, they would probably say, "So? Big deal." But Jewish students said, "That's incredible! That's what the prophets said." As I would go through each prophecy their responses would be the same: "That's incredible!"

I remember sharing these prophecies with one guy who kept saying, "Wow!" Every time I read him something he would say, "Wow . . . wow . . . wow!"

"Do you believe all this?" he finally asked me.

"Yes, I do," I said. "And I celebrate Passover every year with my family in our home."

'Wow," he said for the sixteenth time. "*You* have Passover?"

"That's right," I said.

I have encouraged Jewish neighbors to celebrate Passover. Some of them didn't celebrate it before, and when they found out *we* did, they were jealous. There we were, a Gentile family, excited about the covenants and feasts, about God in His Jewish form, about the Messiah. God says He will make the Jewish people jealous by sharing His salvation with us. It's Paul's theme and my theme, but we need to remember that it's only a temporary situation.

RESTORATION

"For I do not want you, brethren, to be uninformed of this mystery, lest you be wise in your own estimation, that a partial hardening has happened to Israel until the fullness of the Gentiles has come in" (11:25). It's only a partial hardening, not total and not final. Someday the Jewish people will be restored to a relationship with God, and when they are they'll ask the Messiah to return. That's when Christ will come back, and God's plan will be complete.

Speaking to the Gentiles, Paul says, "Quite right, they [the Jews] were broken off for their unbelief, and you stand only by your faith" (11:20, brackets added). The picture is of an olive tree with several branches broken off. The Jewish people are the olive tree, and the broken branches are those who have rejected God. Gentiles who believe in God are then grafted into the tree because of their faith.

"Do not be conceited," Paul warns, "but fear; for if God did not spare the natural branches, neither will He spare you" (11:20-21). If God cut off the Jewish people, who were the natural branches, He would also cut off unfaithful Gentiles who have been grafted in.

Paul's next statement has a lot to say about the nature of God:

Behold then the kindness and severity of God; to those who fell, severity, but to you, God's kindness, if you continue in His kindness; otherwise you also will be cut off. And they also, if they do not continue in their unbelief, will be grafted in; for God is able to graft them in again. For if you were cut off from what is by nature a wild olive tree, and were grafted contrary to nature into a cultivated olive tree, how much more shall these who are the natural branches be grafted into their own olive tree? (11:22-24)

"Behold the kindness and severity of God." We have a tendency to forget one or both of those divine characteristics. When we do, we make the Almighty God of creation and salvation into another god—to make *the* God *a* god.

DISOBEDIENCE, INDIFFERENCE, AND DISTRACTION

Our tendency to try to "demote" God results in three things. The first one is *disobedience*. It is dealt with throughout Romans 9–11 and is equated with unbelief. Paul says we're not looking at, worshiping, and relating to God as God, and that's disobedience.

Our world always moves toward this disobedience, this unbelief. That's why we need to pay attention to and remember the statement, "Behold the kindness and severity of God." There is a balance about God. He has great kindness, a great grace that He pours out on us, but we dare not bask in His kindness and forget His severity. He is God, and He is capable of cutting us off, just as He cut the Jews off.

In *The Lion, the Witch and the Wardrobe*, the first book of the Chronicles of Narnia by C.S. Lewis, the children are talking about the great lion Aslan who represents Jesus Christ. They ask Mr. and Mrs. Beaver about Aslan. "Is He safe?" they ask.

"Oh, no," Mrs. Beaver says. "He's not safe, but He is good."

Later in the story a girl named Polly goes to a well to get some water. Aslan is sitting there with his big paws perched by the bucket. "May I get some water?" Polly asks timidly.

"The water is right here," Aslan says.

Shaking a little, Polly says, "Would you promise not to hurt me?"

"I make no promises," the lion replies. It's His prerogative as God. He has that freedom.

A petrified Polly then asks, "Do you eat girls?"

"I have eaten girls," Aslan says, "and boys and nations and kingdoms."

There God is in all His majesty. Yet we try to demote Him, to disobey Him. We start building up our own works, thinking we can be terrific on our own because we have God's power. God's power can't be taken for granted, and God's kindness and severity can't be separated.

The second thing that our tendency to demote God results in is *indifference* toward God. When we make *the* God *a* god, we become complacent about Him. We're like the little boy in Sunday School whose class was studying about Judgment Day. The teacher was giving a vivid description of what it would be like—thunder, and lightning, hailstorms, the whole earth consumed by fire—when all of a sudden the boy yelled from the back of the room, "Will we get out of school that day?"

A lot of people have that feeling of indifference when it comes to God. It's an attitude that says, "I don't care about that. I just want to know what *I'm* getting out of the deal."

The final thing that results when we make *the* God *a* god is *distraction*. We begin to worship the blessings of God rather than God Himself. I'm always amazed at people who are completely committed to God "when the chips are up" and at those who are committed when the chips are down because they're sure God is going to bail them out. I'm amazed because they're worshiping the blessings of God rather than God Himself. It's so easy to be distracted by His blessings and to let them get between us and Him.

THE TRUE GOD

When *the* God becomes *a* god in our lives, we lose respect for Him and no longer worship Him. We lose interest in Him and no longer walk with Him. That's because we think we can control Him. He becomes our consultant, someone we check with when we want to and don't when we don't want to. We try to make Aslan, the lion, into a kitten, looking for a god of convenience who will cater to our every need and promise not to hurt us.

Either God is God or He is something you can control. If you make Him *a* god, you may be able to control him, but you cannot control *the* God. He's not something you can turn off and on. He is God. He is both kind and severe. He is not safe, but He is good.

The Christian who tries to demote God isn't much better off than the atheist who hopes the Lord won't do anything to disturb his unbelief. When you have a God who won't bother you, who lets you do what you want in your dating, marriage, and family relationships and in your business affairs, you have the same god the atheist has. You may make *the* God *a* god in your head, but He is not *a* god in reality. God is God whether you believe in Him or not, and He is all-powerful whether you acknowledge Him as such or not.

In *Science Speaks* (Moody Press), author Peter Stoner explains the statistical probability of Moses coming up with the eleven steps of creation in the correct scientific order. Imagine that you've taken little tickets, one of which is marked, and stacked them a mile high over the entire North American continent. You stir all those tickets up and then pick out one, hoping it's the marked ticket. The probability that you'll pick the marked ticket at random is the same as the probability that Moses would record the steps of creation in the correct scientific order. But, with God's guidance, Moses did it! That boggles my mind, and God will boggle your mind if you allow Him to be *the* God instead of *a* god.

DON'T MESS AROUND

A man was going to board his plane at the airport. As he was walking to his gate he saw some people standing in a line. Curious, he went over to see what they were waiting for. He watched as they stood one at a time on a big scale that told them their weight and fortune.

The man thought it was dumb, but he was fascinated, so he decided to give it a try. He stepped onto the machine, put his quarter in, and out came a little slip of paper that read, "You are 37 years old, weigh 175 pounds, and are on your way to Chicago." The guy was shocked. He *was* 37, he *did* weigh 175 pounds, and he *was* on his way to Chicago!

But then he thought, *Wait a minute. I bet it says that to everyone, since most people wouldn't be in this terminal unless they were on their way to Chicago.*

So he got back on the machine, put in another quarter, and received another little piece of paper that said, "You are 37 years old, weigh 175 pounds, and are on your way to Chicago."

There, that proves it, he thought. *It says the same thing every time. I'll just get somebody else to do it and that will prove I'm right.* But he couldn't find anyone else to try it.

"OK," he said to himself. "I'll try this one last time." He found another quarter and stepped back onto the machine. Out came the little piece of paper. "You are 37 years old, weigh 175 pounds, and are on your way to Chicago. However, you've messed around so long with this machine that you're going to miss your plane."

I don't know your age, weight, or destination, but I do know that if you mess around with trying to demote *the* God to *a* god, you're going to miss your plane, spiritually speaking. Be aware of your tendency to demote God, which results in disobedience, indifference, and distraction. Pay attention to the kindness and severity of God. Worship Him and walk with Him, recognizing Him as *the* God of the universe, and as such make Him part of every area of your life.

TEN
THE HEAVEN-TO-EARTH CONNECTION

little boy was trying to show off for his dad. He kept throwing a baseball up in the air and saying, "I can hit this ball a mile, Dad. Yep, I'm a hitter, and I can hit this ball a mile." Finally he threw the ball up and took a swing. "Strike one!" he yelled, but it didn't faze him. "I'll hit it this time, Dad. I'll get it this time." He threw the ball up again and swung. "Strike two! Don't worry, Dad," he assured his father. "I'll hit it this time, no problem. I'll hit this ball a mile." Again the little boy threw the ball up and swung. "Strike three, I'm out!" he yelled.

"Dad," he asked, "Do you think maybe I'm supposed to be a pitcher?"

We all strike out sometimes, and we all question who we are and what we're supposed to do. That's part of life—changing, adapting, amd understanding ourselves better. It's also part of our relationship with God. As we become infused with His life, we will change and adapt and become more whole.

But that doesn't happen automatically. We need to keep our earthly lives and our relationship with God in heaven

linked together. When we separate them, we distort Christianity and we put ourselves in danger of over-spiritualization,
of coming across as super-pious. When a person appears to be
super-pious it has nothing to do with how godly he is. It
probably just means he's got his head in the clouds and his
feet in midair.

There's a great saying about this separation: "If you keep
your eye so fixed on heaven that you never look at earth, you
may stumble into hell." Translated another way it might read,
"You may be so heavenly minded that you're no earthly
good." Keeping the heavenly and earthly together is the
underlying theme of Romans 12.

God has provided man with a means for a heaven-to-earth
connection in the person of Jesus Christ, who bridges the
chasm between God and man. Most religions are based on
man's effort to reach God by figuring God out or by behaving
better; Christianity is just the opposite. Christianity is God
reaching down to man to give him life—a more meaningful
life on earth and eternal life in heaven.

Some Christians spend a lot of time talking about the
sweet by-and-by, forgetting about the nasty now-and-now.
We have a life to live in the here and now, and if Christianity
is not radical enough to make a difference here and now, what
good is it? If it's just a ticket to heaven, why bother? We could
pick that up on our way out.

LIFE IN THE HERE AND NOW

I was in a meeting with a group of men, one of whom was a
pastor. "I'm having real difficulty in my church," he said.

"Oh," I said. "What's the difficulty?"

"The difficulty is that once people let me know their
problems, they're too embarrassed to come back. So the
people in our church who have admitted they have problems
don't come back. Do you find that to be true in your church?"

"No," I said, shaking my head. "In fact, I have just the

opposite problem. People don't come to our church to begin with *unless* they have problems."

The pastor looked rather perplexed. "Oh," he said.

Radical Christianity frees us to be who we are, to admit our problems, and to keep coming back. It frees us to resist being squashed into a box and pressured to live as everyone else thinks we should. Christ allows you to be unique. If you're Jewish, radical Christianity adds to your Jewishness; if you're black, it increases your sense of identity as a black person; if you're Asian, it allows you to be fully Asian; if you're a woman, it makes you more of a woman; if you're a man, it makes you more of a man. Radical Christianity sets you free to be who you are. That's why it's unique.

OFFER YOUR BODY

As Paul makes the heaven-to-earth connection in Romans 12, he pulls four heavenly truths down for our earthly living—four steps that we can take to keep the two linked together. The first one is to offer our bodies: "I urge you therefore, brethren, by the mercies of God, to present your bodies a living and holy sacrifice, acceptable to God, which is your spiritual service of worship" (Romans 12:1).

Notice Paul's choice of words. He doesn't say, "I command you," but "I urge you, therefore." Whenever you read a "therefore," look and see what it's there for. Paul is urging us to offer our bodies "by the mercies of God," based on what God has done for us. It's one of the first things that must take place after we enter a relationship with God. We must offer our bodies to Him.

God wants a "living" body. He doesn't want a dead sacrifice like the ones offered in the Old Testament. The trouble with a living sacrifice is that it can crawl off the altar, but that's a risk God is willing to take. He doesn't tie us down or stick a sword in us to make sure we stay. He just asks us to get on the altar because of what He has done for us.

Some people get on the altar and are scared to death that God is going to zap them. Some keep looking over their shoulders. Some keep one foot on the ground just in case things get hot, and some even use the altar as a platform on which to perform. The important thing is that we get on—alive—as an offering.

Once we have offered our bodies, Paul says, our sacrifice is holy and acceptable to God. Making our bodies holy and acceptable is *God's* part; presenting them to God is *our* part. It's our "spiritual service of worship." That phrase has been found in recent archeological digs to have been used as a liturgy in rites of magic. A lot of people think a formal church liturgy is necessary in order to worship God. Paul says that in order to worship God you need to give the Lord your life, to give Him yourself and say, "God, I want You to take me and use me in other people's lives." That is your personal liturgy.

I grew up in a very strict church and I rebelled strongly against its rules and regulations. On Sunday morning I was a model child, and the rest of the week I was a menace. It was a case of sowing wild oats all week and then praying on Sunday for a crop failure. I kept "offering my body to God" constantly. When I went to camp we would sit around the campfire as the counselors challenged us to give our lives to God.

Good grief, I would think. *Not again.* But I would throw my stick into the fire along with everyone else and say, "OK, here I am again." Then a few hours later I'd be gone and back into trouble.

At church I would walk down the aisle at the end of the service, but before the night was over I would usually get into trouble again. Finally I added these experiences up: I had offered my body to God forty-three times! Because nothing ever "happened," I figured God just wasn't interested in my body. I know now that He *was* interested, but that offering our bodies is only the first step in the heaven-to-earth connection.

OVERHAUL YOUR MIND

Right on the heels of the urging to offer our bodies comes the word *and*. This little word puts together what precedes and what follows. "And do not be conformed to this world, but be transformed by the renewing of your mind, that you may prove what the will of God is, that which is good and acceptable and perfect" (12:2). That is, don't be forced into the mold of this world, into its shackles of conformity. Be totally changed by overhauling your mind. After we have offered our bodies, step two is overhauling our minds.

We humans are creatures of conformity. We want to be like everyone else and not stand out in the crowd. Have you ever been the last person to get on an elevator that was packed so tight no one could even scratch his nose? What did you do? You quickly wiggled yourself around so that you faced the door and fit in with everyone else. Spiritually speaking, don't press yourself into the world's mold. Be uniquely, freely you.

The only way you can be uniquely, freely yourself is "by the renewing of your mind." The word *renew* means to " grow up fresh," and the only thing I know that will grow our minds up fresh is God's Word. By meditating on Scripture and overhauling our minds with it, we can learn the truth that will set us free. Then we "may prove," or put to the test, "what the will of God is, that which is good and acceptable and perfect."

OBTAIN A SERVANT'S HEART

The third step in the heaven-to-earth connection is to obtain a servant's heart. "For through the grace given to me I say to every man among you not to think more highly of himself than he ought to think; but to think so as to have sound judgment, as God has allotted to each a measure of faith" (12:3). Most movements that are full of pious people try to get you to be perfect, or at least to think of yourself as perfect. They try to get you to think more highly of yourself—the exact opposite of what Paul says to do.

Jesus didn't spend much time with people who were pious and pretended to be perfect. He spent His time with people who didn't have it all together, who were having problems, who were in trouble, who were in need of what He has to offer. Come to think of it, Jesus spent His time with the kinds of people who come to our church!

Why are you not to think more highly of yourself than you ought? Because of God's grace. When you came into a relationship with God, He poured out His grace—His unmerited favor—on you. He cleaned your slate, emptied the garbage out of your life, erased your guilt, and forgave your sins—past, present, and future. He continues to pour out His grace on you as you need it, and you *do* need it. You don't have it all together, and what you *do* have you have only because of God's grace.

It used to be that when you asked people how they were doing, about the only answer you ever got was, "Fine." Now when you ask people, "How are you doing?" they often tell you! I think it's great that people today are willing to tell it like it is, rather than act as though it isn't. We don't have our acts together, and we need God's grace. If we were all honest, if we all took off our masks and quit performing, it would be clear that a lot of us aren't doing very well. We all have times when we're not doing well, when we're having problems in our marriages, with our kids, in our businesses, with friends, neighbors, whatever.

There's a bumper sticker that says, "Reality is only for those who can't cope with drugs." Coping with reality *is* difficult, because *life* is difficult. It's much easier to put on airs and pretend than to face life head-on, and the games people play in religious circles are particularly evasive. I overheard someone at a pastors' conference say, "Well, of course I'm preaching through Isaiah verse by verse." I wanted to ask him, "Does anyone *care* that you're preaching through Isaiah verse by verse?"

We all put on airs. We all want to pump ourselves up a

little and imagine ourselves rising above the crowd. Paul says in Romans, "Don't do it. Make the heaven-to-earth connection, live in reality, and tell it like it is. Admit where you are, how you feel, and what you're doing, and if something needs to be changed, resolve to take care of it. Obtain a servant's heart and don't think more highly of yourself than you ought to think."

OPERATE IN THE BODY OF BELIEVERS

"For just as we have many members in one body and all the members do not have the same function, so we, who are many, are one body in Christ, and individually members one of another" (12:4-5). The fourth step in the heaven-to-earth connection is to operate in the body of believers. We need one another. We need older people and younger people. We need people who don't have it as together as we do and people who have it *more* together than we do. We need each other desperately, and it's always a two-way deal—I need you and you need me.

> And since we have gifts that differ according to the grace given to us, let each exercise them accordingly: if prophecy, according to the proportion of his faith; if service, in his serving; or he who teaches, in his teaching; or he who exhorts, in his exhortation; he who gives, with liberality; he who leads, with diligence; he who shows mercy, with cheerfulness (12:6-8).

I need you and you need me because we each have different gifts, different God-given abilities for helping people and building up the body. They are undeserved blessings of God, and we are to use them for His service. Maybe your gift is prophecy—which is not necessarily prediction, but challenging people to action. Or it may be exhorting, or encouraging people or showing mercy—cheering people up when they feel bad.

Whatever your gift is, Paul says, "Exercise it!" He could have said, "OK, Christians, when you find out what your gift is, be very careful how you use it so that you don't screw up." Instead he says, "Operate in the body of believers." Whatever your gift is, go for it. Don't be afraid to exercise your gift, fearing you might make a mistake and somebody might look at you funny or laugh at you.

The best way I know to operate in the body of believers, and the *only* way if your church is large, is to get involved in a small group. In our church we have what we call mini-churches, and they are the life of the congregation. Individuals meet in homes, according to the geographical area they live in, to share their needs and exercise their gifts together. I hope Sunday morning is an enjoyable and encouraging time too, but to truly operate in the body of believers we must be involved in individuals' lives—getting to know them, caring for them, and sharing our gifts with them.

QUALITIES OF THE CONNECTION

Having given us four steps toward keeping our heavenly relationship with God and our earthly lives linked together, Paul lists some qualities to strive for in that connection:

Let love be without hypocrisy. Abhor what is evil; cleave to what is good. Be devoted to one another in brotherly love; give preference to one another in honor; not lagging behind in diligence, fervent in spirit, serving the Lord; rejoicing in hope, persevering in tribulation, devoted to prayer, contributing to the needs of the saints, practicing hospitality. Bless those who persecute you; bless and curse not. Rejoice with those who rejoice and weep with those who weep. Be of the same mind toward one another; do not be haughty in mind, but associate with the lowly. Do not be wise in your own estimation. Never pay back evil for evil to anyone. Respect what is right in the sight of all men. If possible, so far as it depends on you, be at peace with all men. Never take your own revenge, beloved, but leave room for the wrath of God, for it is written, "Vengeance is Mine, I will repay," says the Lord. "But if your enemy is hungry, feed him, and if he is thirsty, give him a drink; for in so doing you will heap burning coals upon his head." Do not be overcome by evil, but overcome evil with good (12:9-21).

The instruction Paul gives is motivating: "Be devoted to one another . . . give preference to one another." Try, he says, to outdo one another in giving honor. His advice is strong: "Bless those who persecute you; bless and curse not." It is realistic: "So far as it depends on you, be at peace with all men." It is smart: "Never take your own revenge . . . leave room for the wrath of God." In other words, scoot over when you're attacked, because God can take care of it much better than you can.

Paul's teaching is also compassionate: "If your enemy is hungry, feed him, and if he is thirsty, give him a drink." And finally, it is human: "In so doing you will heap burning coals upon his head."

How can we make that heaven-to-earth connection? The first two steps, offering our bodies and overhauling our minds, require a commitment to God. They are saying, "God, I'll let You use everything I've got. It's all Yours."

When I was a campus minister, I knew a student who started meditating on Romans 12. When he got to this part he said to me, "Do you know what I think this means? I think this means God wants every part of my body." He told me he was giving God his body part by part. "God," he would pray, "I've got this tongue that's not too terrific sometimes; I mean, it says some pretty awful things, so I want to give it to You. And my ears, God—what they've been hearing lately has been really rotten, so I'd like to give them to You too. Speaking of senses, I've been sticking my nose into places where it shouldn't be stuck again, so You'd better take it too. And these legs, Lord—they don't seem to be taking me to the right kinds of places. And my eyes . . ." And on he went, giving every part of his body to God. He knew that offering your body and overhauling your mind involve a commitment to God.

The last two steps in making the heaven-to-earth connection—obtaining a servant's heart and operating in the body of believers—deal with our commitments to others, to the community. The community includes both believers and nonbelievers, and we are to relate to both of them.

I summarize it this way: *The heaven-to-earth connection requires that you celebrate the grace of God in your life.* God's grace is woven all the way through Romans 12: "I urge you therefore, brethren, by the mercies of God"—by what God has done for you, by His grace—"to present your bodies" (v. 1); "For through the grace given to me . . . as God has allotted to each a measure of faith" (v. 3); "And since we have gifts that differ according to the grace given to us" (v. 6). Each of the steps we take in making the connection is a celebration of the grace of God. A celebration is like a cheer. It's glorifying God, reflecting Him in our lifestyle and giving our all to the God who has given us His grace.

Do you find it hard to celebrate God's grace? See if this story doesn't help you.

A little boy prayed and prayed to receive a sled for Christmas, but when Christmas came, there was no sled. There was also no snow. The boy knew his family was poor, but he thought maybe if he prayed for the whole next year somehow he would be able to get a sled. It did snow three or four times that year, but when Christmas came again there was still no sled. Undaunted, the little boy continued to pray every night that God would give him a sled.

One afternoon in March the boy's father walked past a hardware store that had recently burned down. A few things that had been salvaged from the fire lay on the sidewalk, free for the taking. One of the things was a sled. Knowing his little boy had wanted a sled for so long, the father took it home to him.

The little boy was so excited! "God has answered my prayers!" he said. Even though it had never snowed there in March, he told his parents, "Now I'm going to pray for snow."

That night it got unusually cold, and before the sun rose the snow started to fall. When the little boy woke up the next morning and saw the snow coming down, he grabbed his sled and headed out the door in his pajamas. "Attaboy, God!" he yelled. "You're doing great!"

That's what we need to be saying and reflecting in our lifestyles—a celebration of God's grace.

Radical Christianity starts with God reaching down to man, giving him meaning and purpose right now as well as for eternity. We need to respond by receiving and celebrating God's grace, making the heaven-to-earth connection, and relating to God and other believers. We need to offer our bodies, overhaul our minds, obtain a servant's heart, operate in the body of believers . . . and cheer God on!

ELEVEN
THE CHURCH:
A MOVEMENT,
NOT A MONUMENT

he Book of Romans occupies a strategic position in the New Testament. First, it presents Christianity from beginning to end—justification, santification, and glorification—and second, it was written to the church at Rome.

The latter is important because Rome was the heart of the civilized world, the capital of the Roman Empire. Rome's more than 1 million inhabitants lived in peace and were therefore open to new influences. Though the majority of its residents were slaves, and though opulence and squalor coexisted there, Rome was wealthy, powerful, influential, and a center of diplomacy and trade. The church there was well known throughout the rest of the world and because of its position, it played a key role to giving Christianity to the rest of the world.

There are also places today that play key roles in the spread of Christianity. One strategic area in the United States is Washington, D.C. What happens there, as far as the Gospel is concerned, has far-reaching effects. Another strategic area is Southern California. Somehow whatever we start here—good and bad—grows quickly and makes its way across the country.

We originate, enlarge, and then export all kinds of things.

The important issue in any strategic area, and the issue Paul addresses in Romans 13–16, is the direction Christianity is going. What is the church in Rome, or Washington, D.C. or Southern California becoming? Is it growing into a movement . . . or a monument?

MARKERS OF DEATH

So much of Christianity is filled with monuments, with brick and mortar, with people who are stationary and stuck. The church has become like a football game with 22 players on the field who are badly in need of rest and 76,000 fans in the bleachers who are badly in need of exercise. Paul is trying in Romans 13–16 to get us away from being uninvolved, passive spectators, toward being involved, active participants. He wants to move us from being dead to God toward being alive to God.

Too many churches in our culture have built monuments—buildings that are beautiful on the outside but without life on the inside. Churches need to be functional and aesthetically pleasing, but we must take great pains not to create monstrosities that become markers of death to the believers who worship there.

Our church is a hospital for sinners, not a home for saints. We allow only those who *don't* have it all together to attend. I mentioned that fact several years ago at a praise gathering in Indianapolis, and afterward three women came up to me. One of them said, "Do you believe that Christians sin?"

"Yes," I answered, "I do."

As it turned out, they didn't!

"What is it you *do* then," I asked, "when you blow it?"

When they told me, I nearly died. It was all I could do to keep my composure.

"We make *mistakes*," they said. "But we don't *sin*."

It doesn't matter how you label things, or what "lodge"

you're a member of—denominational or nondenominational. What does matter is whether your church is a movement or a monument.

LIVE IT OUT ON THIS PLANET

Having urged us to offer our bodies, overhaul our minds, obtain a servant's heart, and operate in the body of believers, Paul now takes his heaven-to-earth connection one step further in Romans 13. He presents the first characteristic of a movement: it must be lived out on this planet. "Let every person be in subjection to the governing authorities. For there is no authority except from God, and those which exist are established by God" (Romans 13:1).

This is a difficult teaching to digest, to understand, and to coordinate with other teachings. It's also difficult because we have a hard time believing that God sets up and removes authority.

THE REALMS OF AUTHORITY

There are four basic realms of authority. One is government. Because God uses government to keep our world in order, we are to submit to it in the fear of the Lord. The second realm is employer-employee relationship; Peter says we are to submit to our employers as to the Lord (1 Peter 2:18). The home is the third realm of authority. There the wife is to submit to her husband in the fear of the Lord, not because he's all-knowing and all-wise, but to eliminate chaos and provide order. The fourth realm is the church. There believers are to submit to its leaders, to the governing body, again so that order can be maintained.

Authority is a neutral vehicle to counteract chaos and establish order so that things can get done. Governing authorities have been established for two purposes: to punish evil and reward good.

Therefore he who resists authority has opposed the ordinance of God; and they who have opposed will receive condemnation upon themselves. For rulers are not a cause of fear for good behavior, but for evil. Do you want to have no fear of authority? Do what is good, and you will have praise from the same; for it is a minister of God to you for good. But if you do what is evil, be afraid; for it does not bear the sword for nothing; for it is a minister of God, an avenger who brings wrath upon the one who practices evil. Wherefore it is necessary to be in subjection, not only because of wrath, but also for conscience' sake. For because of this you also pay taxes, for rulers are servants of God, devoting themselves to this very thing. Render to all what is due them: tax to whom tax is due; custom to whom custom; fear to whom fear; honor to whom honor (13:2-7).

In other words, the Christian and the church must live in the real world and submit to the governing authorities.

The question that usually comes up at this point is, "What if one governing authority moves into the area of another?" If the government starts taking over the home and telling you when you can have children and when you can't, you have an obligation to disobey it. If it moves into the church and says you can't read your Bible or even own one, you have an obligation to disobey it. If the church comes along and tells you whom you can and can't marry, you have an obligation to disobey it. When you rebel against authority that's in line with the Bible, you're in trouble; but when one authority tries to take over another's jurisdiction, you must disobey.

NEIGHBORS

From authority Paul goes on to talk about neighbors:

Owe nothing to anyone except to love one another; for he who loves his neighbor has fulfilled the Law.

For this, "You shall not commit adultery, you shall not murder, you shall not steal, you shall not covet," and if there is any other commandment, it is summed up in this saying, "You shall love your neighbor as yourself." Love does no wrong to a neighbor; love therefore is the fulfillment of the Law. . . . But put on the Lord Jesus Christ, and make no provision for the flesh in regard to its lusts (13:8-10, 14).

Paul is dealing with our public and private lives, reiterating the first characteristic of a movement: the Christian life can't be lived in the heavenlies or on some spiritual cloud. We have to live it on this planet, submitting to the government and loving our neighbors.

THE GREAT ESCAPE

Lots of people try to escape living out their Christianity on this planet. That's what the Gnostics, described in chapter 6, attempted to do. They tried to escape by accumulating more and more knowledge, but because it was only head knowledge, Christianity never affected their lives.

It breaks my heart that people are still living that Gnostic heresy and that pastors, some very good friends of mine, are still teaching it. One pastor I've known for years teaches Greek as no one else I know teaches Greek. He goes deep and stays deep; in fact, he never comes up for air. His whole thing is to take it in, store it up, get it into your head. He has six Bible studies a week which he requires the members of his church to attend. If people don't attend all six, they can't be members of the church. That's one sure way to cut down on church growth. It's an escape.

Other people try to escape living out their Christianity on this planet by using the "sovereignty of God" extreme. God *is* sovereign, but He has given man certain responsibilities. This extreme teaches only God's sovereignty. Man doesn't have to do anything, according to this view. God will take care of everything. Whatever God does gets done, and whatever He doesn't do doesn't get done. Man doesn't do anything—except escape.

LIVE IT OUT WITH PEOPLE

Romans 14 and 15 deal with the second characteristic of a movement—it must be lived out with people. This is a tough one for me, and for most of us, because there are no exceptions. It doesn't say, "Pick out the people you like and live the Christian life with them." It says, "Live the Christian life with people—those you like and those you aren't especially fond of."

ACCEPT THOSE WHO ARE WEAK

There are four aspects to living out Christianity with people. The first is to accept those who are weak, those who, for their own reasons, have chosen not to exercise their freedom in some area.

"Now accept the one who is weak in faith, but not for the purpose of passing judgment on his opinions. One man has faith that he may eat all things, but he who is weak eats vegetables only" (14:1-2). That doesn't mean vegetarians are weak. Paul is talking about food that has been sacrificed to idols, not about diet and health.

"Let not him who eats regard with contempt him who does not eat, and let not him who does not eat judge him who eats, for God has accepted him" (14:3). The problem was that weaker believers had a hang-up about eating meat that had been sacrificed to idols, not because it was right or wrong, but for their own spiritual reasons. Some people today have hang-ups about going to the movies or drinking alcoholic beverages, not because it's right or wrong, but for their own spiritual reasons.

If you have a hang-up about doing something, don't do it. If you have faith that you may do something, do it. "Nothing is unclean in itself" (14:14). But if you are free, don't have contempt on those who aren't. Don't parade your freedom in front of them or try to push it down their throats, saying "Come on, have a drink. God says it's OK and Paul says it's OK, so don't be so legalistic. Go ahead, indulge yourself." If you are *not* free, don't judge those who are and are doing what you don't feel free to do.

Several years ago my wife Carol and I went back to the Midwest to "rescue" an organization in which I had grown up. This organization believed that what you *don't* do is more important than what you *do,* and they were known for what they didn't do. Having realized that Scripture says we're free, and being free ourselves, Carol and I went back to "free" them.

We came waving a red flag that read, "You are free," but it didn't take long to realize that the people in that organization didn't *want* to be free. They were perfectly happy in their shackles. I had contempt on them when I left there, and I shook the dirt off my feet and walked out. I judged them, and I was angry that they had the nerve to judge me.

Then I read that I wasn't to have contempt on those who aren't free. "Let not him who eats regard with contempt him who does not eat, and let not him who does not eat judge him who eats, for God has accepted him. Who are you to judge the servant of another? To his own master he stands or falls; and stand he will, for the Lord is able to make him stand. One man regards one day above another, another regards every day alike. Let each man be fully convinced in his own mind" (14:3-5).

The specific reference here is to the Sabbath. Some people believe Sunday is the day you don't do anything but go to church and out to brunch. I've never figured out where they get the "out to brunch" part, but somehow they've managed to sneak that in. If you have that conviction, that's great. Just remember that no day is holier than any other day, brunch or no brunch.

The reason for accepting those who are weak is summarized in this verse: "So then each one of us shall give account of himself to God" (14:12). We will stand before God and answer to Him for the use of our freedom.

KEEP FROM OFFENDING ONE ANOTHER

The second aspect of living out Christianity with other people is found later in Romans 14:

> Therefore let us not judge one another any more, but rather determine this—not to put an obstacle or a stumbling-block in a brother's way. I know and am convinced in the Lord Jesus that nothing is unclean in itself; but to him who thinks anything to be unclean, to him it is unclean. For if because of food your brother is hurt, you are no longer walking according to love. Do not destroy with your food him for whom Christ died. Therefore do not let what is for you a good thing be spoken of as evil; for the kingdom of God is not eating and drinking, but righteousness and peace and joy in the Holy Spirit. For he who in this way serves Christ is acceptable to God and approved by men (14:13-18).

We need to take care that what we do doesn't offend people. What we're doing may not be wrong, but it's wrong to do it if it offends someone. It's a matter of being sensitive to people and sensible in our actions.

GLORIFY GOD TOGETHER

Romans 15 presents the third aspect of living out our Christianity with other people.

> Now we who are strong ought to bear the weaknesses of those without strength and not just please our-

selves. Let each of us please his neighbor for his good,
to his edification. . . . that with one accord you may
with one voice glorify the God and Father of our Lord
Jesus Christ. Wherefore, accept one another, just as
Christ also accepted us to the glory of God (15: 1-2,
6-7).

As we look around at the Christians with whom we have to
live, with whom we are supposed to glorify God, it can be
pretty discouraging. We have to live with believers who are
absolutely obnoxious, who constantly misunderstand us. We
have to live with those who continually judge us, have contempt on us, or offend us. We have to live with Christians
who have problems and with those who don't. We have to
live with and glorify God with a *mess*—but it's an essential
part of the movement!

BE PEOPLE ORIENTED

Though looking at Christians as a whole can be discouraging,
looking at them individually can be encouraging. That's what
Paul does in Romans 16 as he presents the fourth aspect of
living out our Christianity with others. As he greets twenty-
six people in five house churches, he shows us the beauty in
the body of believers.

"I commend to you our sister Phoebe," he begins, "who is
a servant of the church which is at Cenchrea; that you receive
her in the Lord in a manner worthy of the saints, and that you
help her in whatever matter she may have need of you; for she
herself has also been a helper of many, and of myself as well"
(16:1-2). Phoebe was what I call a "pro status" woman. She
had an official position in the church, with an official title, and
she ministered to people like crazy.

Next Paul asks the church at Rome to greet Prisca, or
Priscilla, and Aquila. They were probably married and were
"fellow-workers in Christ Jesus, who for my life risked their
own necks, to whom not only do I give thanks, but also all the

churches of the Gentiles; also greet the church that is in their house" (16:3-5). Priscilla and Aquila had a house church, somewhat similar to the mini-churches we have in our congregation. In New Testament times that was the only kind of church there was.

Paul then greets a long list of people. Notice their varied backgrounds.

Greet Epaenetus [a slave], my beloved, who is the first convert of Christ from Asia. Greet Mary, who has worked hard for you. Greet Andronicus and Junias, my kinsmen, and my fellow-prisoners, who are outstanding among the apostles, who also were in Christ before me. Greet Ampliatus [a member of the imperial household], my beloved in the Lord. . . . Greet Apelles, the approved in Christ.

Greet those who are of the household of Aristobulus [a member of Hero's household]. Greet Herodian, my kinsman. Greet those of the household of Narcissus [a very wealthy man], who are in the Lord. Greet Tryphaena and Tryphosa [probably twins], workers in the Lord. Greet Persis [a slave] the beloved, who has worked hard in the Lord. Greet Rufus [who may have been a black man and the son of Simon the Cyrenian], a choice man in the Lord, also his mother and mine. Greet Asyncritus, Phlegon, Hermes [a slave], Patrobas, Hermas and the brethren with them. Greet Philologus [also a member of the imperial household] and Julia, Nereus and his sister, and Olympas, and all the saints who are with them. Greet one another with a holy kiss. All the churches of Christ greet you (Rom. 16:10-16, brackets added).

Every variety Heinz has to offer is listed in Paul's greeting: Men, women, minorities, rich, poor, aristocrats, slaves, people of many professions. All are gathered together in the body of Christ. Paul makes it clear by his example that we are to be people oriented as we live out our Christianity on Planet

Earth. The radical Christian lifestyle must be people oriented, not program oriented. Whenever the program gets ahead of the people, the church becomes a monument instead of a movement.

Throughout his greeting Paul describes the people in the Roman church as hard workers. They served one another. In 1 Thessalonians Paul indicates that those he has served are his crown: "For who is our hope or joy or crown of exultation? Is it not even you, in the presence of our Lord Jesus at His coming? For you are our glory and joy" (1 Thes. 2:19-20). Looking around at the people in Thessalonica, Paul saw his crown of rejoicing. Those he had served would be his reward when Christ returned.

Forget the diamonds and emeralds and whatever else is in heaven. *People* are our crown when we get to the Judgment Seat. As we minister to people, introducing them to the Lord and helping them to mature in Christ, they become our crown of rejoicing. The Christians we have to live with can be a mess, but when we serve them we have an opportunity to transform them into "our hope or joy or crown of exultation." Not a bad deal!

LIVE IT OUT IN THE POWER OF GOD
There's something else that characterizes the church as a movement. It's the power of God.

Connecting with that power starts back in Romans 12, where Paul urges us to present our bodies to God and transform our lives by renewing our minds. Once we have done that, God gives us the power to live the Christian life. "I'm going to give you the power to have gifts so that you can effectively minister to people. I'm going to give you the power to be gracious and kind to people when they insult you. I'm going to give you the power to submit to authorities and love your neighbors, to accept the person who isn't free and the person who is. I'm going to give you the power to get

along with *all* the people in the body." When we give ourselves to Him, God gives us that kind of power.

Romans 15 also indicates the presence of God's power.

Now may the God of hope fill you with all joy and
peace in believing, that you may abound in hope by
the power of the Holy Spirit. . . . For I will not
presume to speak of anything except what Christ has
accomplished through me, resulting in the obedience
of the Gentiles by word and deed, in the power of
signs and wonders, in the power of the Spirit; so that
from Jerusalem and round about as far as Illyricum
[present-day Yugoslavia] I have fully preached the
Gospel of Christ (Romans 15:13, 18-19, brackets
added).

When God's power is present, people are filled with joy and
peace. Slaves are lifted up, and people in high positions count
on God rather than relying on themselves. God's power
makes a *difference* in people's lives. It's the key to a movement;
in fact, it's the *definition* of a movement.

*A movement takes place where God is making a difference in
your life now!* Not several years ago, not in a few weeks, but
now. Not a nudge, not a dent, but a *difference.*

I'm frequently asked why I don't write a book on church
growth. "Because it would only be a page long," I reply. All I
would have to say on that subject could be put on one page,
probably in one sentence: *A movement takes place where God is
making a difference in people's lives now.*

THE RADICAL DIFFERENCE

Let me ask you a very difficult question. Where is God
making a difference in your life right now? It's one thing to
say, "Oh, yes, now that God's in my life things are different."
It's something else to say, "This is where God is making a
difference in my life *today.*"

Most of the time we're willing to stand on the sidelines

and cheer, but we're extremely cautious when it comes to actually getting involved and letting God make a difference. We pray for people who are starving, but we're not willing to feed them. We're happy to ask God for a school building in an African village, but we're not willing to go build it. We remember those who are unloved and lonely and desperate in our prayers, but we're not willing to love them and be a friend to them and encourage them. Being a spectator is a cinch, but becoming a participant involves a commitment.

Our hesitation to get involved in others' lives results from our hesitation to let God be involved in our own lives. We're willing to go along, but we don't really expect to get anywhere. We act as though nothing's going to happen when we get involved with Him. We're like the people who'd been experiencing a drought for months and came to a church meeting to pray for rain. As the pastor looked out he saw all the members there, dressed in their best duds, but not one had an umbrella.

God wants us to pray *and* carry an umbrella. He wants to be involved in our lives, to give us His power so we can live the Christian life, be part of a movement, and have lives that are different now.

If you're a Christian and you want God to make a difference in your life right now, it's as simple as A B C. First of all, *ask* Him to make your life different. "Let your requests be made known to God. And the peace of God, which surpasses all comprehension, shall guard your hearts and your minds in Christ Jesus" (Phil. 4:6-7). That's a promise from God, and what God says He'll do, He does. I dare say most Christians haven't tried that promise. No matter what area you're struggling with, ask, "God, will You make a difference in my life now?"

Next, *believe* God is able and wants to do what you've asked Him. God wants us to be part of His movement. He wants to provide the rain for our umbrellas, but He can't if we won't even walk out the door and give Him a chance!

Finally, *celebrate* what God is doing in your life. Reflect on it, talk about it, express it. Get excited about the difference He is making.

A minister was out playing golf with a new convert. The new convert swung through, missed the ball, and began cussing up a storm. The minister said, "Hey, you're a Christian now, don't talk like that."

When the minister had finished working him over, the new convert said, "Oh, Reverend, don't get so upset. I swear a little, and you pray a little, but neither one of us means a darn thing by it."

I'm afraid that's the way we are. We pray a little bit, but do we mean anything by it? Do we really want God to make a difference in our lives?

If you want to be a part of a movement, not a monument, ask God to make a difference in your life. Believe He is able to make a difference. And celebrate the difference—today!

Presbyterian had just arrived in heaven, and Saint Peter was showing him around. They were talking and laughing and singing as they went on their way, when suddenly they came upon a group of tents. "Shhhhhhh!" said Peter.

"What do you mean, Shhhhhhh?" said the Presbyterian. "This is *heaven*. What happened to making a joyful noise and singing a new song and all that?"

"Nothing," explained Peter. "It's just that those are the Baptists over there in those tents, and they think they're the only ones here!"

UNRADICAL CHRISTIANITY

Arnold Toynbee said that people have not rejected Christianity, but a poor caricature of it. Because so many people think they have the only key to heaven's gate, Christianity has been distorted. Christians are usually quick to pick up on the major cults being propagated these days, and many are even prepared to do battle with them, but Christians often practice the same distortions themselves. A lot of churches have become cults, and a lot of Christianity has become a cult, because what is being preached and practiced is a distortion of real, radical Christianity.

Believers and nonbelievers respond differently to the distortion. Believers buy this poor imitation of Christianity, move into an embalmed state because of it, and then proceed to turn off everyone with whom they come in contact. Nonbelievers balk at it. They balk at the cultish words and ways of the caricature, reject it completely, and then keep away from anything that smells like it.

I don't blame the nonbelievers, and I commend them for their perceptiveness. They agree with the Indian who went to listen to a famous preacher. When asked what he thought of the sermon, the Indian said, "Big wind, loud thunder, no rain."

Dwight Moody, the great evangelist, began taking a group of indigent boys he was working with to church with him. After he had done so for several Sundays, he spoke to the minister about becoming a member of the church. The minister said Moody would first have to be examined by a board.

The board didn't want Moody there because of the boys he was bringing. The "little heathens" were messing up their neat little meetings. So, they asked Moody to pray for a month and see if God encouraged him to join their church.

The board thought they had seen the last of Moody, but one month later he was back. "Well," they said, "did God encourage you to join this church or not?"

"He encouraged me to *try,*" answered Moody. "He also mentioned that *He* had been trying to get in for the last twenty-five years."

Like the members of that board, much of Christianity has left God out. It has gathered up the "good stuff," gotten together just the "right people," and formed a tight little group—so tight there isn't room for God, much less for a group of indigent boys.

Jesus warned us in the Parable of the Wheat and Tares (Matt. 13:24-30) about sorting things out for ourselves. He said there would be wheat—genuine believers—planted in the field. In the same field there would be tares—false believers. Those who were listening to Him said, "Shouldn't we go out and pull up all the tares?"

"No," Jesus said in effect. "If you do you'll also pull up some of the wheat. Let Me take care of the sorting. You just relate to people where they are and keep relaying the truth."

MAJORS, NOT MINORS

Probably the most common way we distort Christianity is by majoring in the minors and minoring in the majors. Some of us believe all the speakers, teachers, and gurus, who come along without ever comparing what they say with the Bible. That's how we end up emphasizing things that God doesn't—majoring in the minors. We also disregard the things God wants us to emphasize—minoring in the majors.

Jesus addressed that issue in the Gospel of Mark: "Rightly did Isaiah prophesy of you hypocrites, as it is written, 'This people honors Me with their lips [outwardly], but their heart is far from Me. But in vain do they worship Me [inwardly empty], teaching as doctrines the precepts of men.' Neglecting the commandment of God, you hold to the tradition of men" (Mark 7:6-8, brackets added).

When the Scripture clearly states something, it's absolute, and it should be taught that way. But lots of things in Scripture are open to opinion, and one person's opinion can be just as good as another's. That's why opinions can be so destructive.

For example, some people say you should use a lot of water for baptism. Others say dunking isn't necessary; just dip those converts. Some say you ought to sprinkle, since it's quicker and less trouble. Others say pouring is the only way to go. We get so involved with the way we do things that we end up majoring in the minors. It doesn't make any difference whether we dunk, dip, sprinkle, pour, squirt, or dry clean because no matter how we do it, it's not our deal. It's God's deal, and we just happen to be participating in it.

When my wife Carol and I were involved in campus ministry, we saw lots of students trust the Lord and grow with Him in a dynamic way. We had to fill out reports indicating how many people had trusted the Lord, what they were doing now, and who was going into the ministry. As we filled out report after report we begin to think, "Wow, we're pretty cool. We're doing a terrific job."

The further we got from that situation, however, the more we realized that we had just happened to be there when those people came through. We were stationed there for God, and He brought each individual to us. I'm thankful for that experience, and that God is the One who stations us places and sends us people. There's nowhere we can go and nothing we can do to manufacture it. We just get to participate in it.

We also major in the minors when it comes to personal experiences. People love to share how God spoke to them here, gave them a vision there, or zapped them with this or that. A student came up to me after the Expo '72 conference in Dallas and said, "Guess what? While I was sitting in the Cotton Bowl I had a vision. God came down and Jesus spoke to me. I knew I was a nonbeliever, and I accepted Christ right there! What do you think of that?"

"I think that's wonderful," I said. "Did you accept Jesus as your personal Saviour?"

"Yes," she answered. "I did."

"That's wonderful," I repeated.

"Well, what do I do now?" she asked.

"Don't patent it," I said. "Keep that experience between you and God, and don't expect it to happen again."

What usually happens when people have an uncommon experience is that they want to have it again. They want other people to have it too, so they start preaching about it and writing pamphlets on it and try to patent and sell it. God works in lots of different ways, but when we start emphasizing our experiences, we end up majoring in the minors.

As Jesus told the scribes and Pharisees,

You nicely set aside the commandment of God in order to keep your tradition. For Moses said, "Honor your father and your mother"; and, "He who speaks evil of father or mother, let him be put to death"; but you say, "If a man says to his father or his mother, anything of mine you might have been helped by is Corban, (that is to say, given to God), you no longer permit him to do anything for his father or his mother; thus invalidating the Word of God by your tradition which you have handed down; and you do many things such as that (Mark 7:9-13).

PRECEPTS VS. PRINCIPLES

There are absolutes in the Bible—things that are true for everyone whether or not anyone believes them. There are also things that are nonabsolutes—things that are not true for everyone, but which some try to *make* absolute because they believe them so deeply. Those who do so distort Christianity. They try to make principles into precepts.

A precept would be a speed limit sign on the freeway. It's the law, and it's absolute. You are not to go over 55 miles per hour. A principle would be a "Drive Carefully" sign. It's still the law, but it has to be interpreted by each driver according to the particular situation. Everyone is to drive carefully, but that will mean different things to different people at different times.

The Bible is full of precepts, things that are nonnegotiable and unchangeable, but it is also full of principles. For example, "Train up a child in the way he should go, even when he is old he will not depart from it" (Prov. 22:6). The precept is to parent your children, but the principle of training them up can vary greatly. I have fun in my parenthood seminar showing people how differently they treat their children, because their children are so different. All they need to do is stay within the principle, "parent properly."

PERSONAL CONVICTIONS

Not only do Christians try to make absolutes out of principles, but they also try to make them out of personal convictions. For instance, you may have a personal conviction before God that you should not drink any alcohol at all. If you want to tell other people about your personal conviction, that's fine; when you start to legislate it, that's not fine. It's making absolutes of nonabsolutes, and it's distorting Christianity.

Much of the time our personal convictions are about something we don't like or can't do anyway. I had a personal conviction about beer for a long time. I couldn't stand it, not even the smell of it, so I just found a verse and started preaching against it. "You shouldn't drink beer!" I said. Personal convictions, for whatever reason, are fine, but when they are imposed on others, they become a distortion.

NOT PERFECT; IN PROCESS

We also drift away from real, radical Christianity when we buy into the distortion of perfectionism. Everyone is reaching for perfection, trying to look, be, and act perfect. We want a perfect mate, perfect children, a perfect job, a perfect house, perfect friends. We want *life* to be perfect! The world knows there is no such thing, but for some reason it expects Christians to be the exception to the rule. Some Christians also expect that of themselves.

Christians are not perfect—that is a distortion. But they *are* in process—and that is the distinctive of Christianity. I like the bumper sticker that says, "Christians aren't perfect—just forgiven." We are under construction, in the process of growing and changing.

A man who didn't recognize this came up to me one Sunday after the service. He said, "I don't buy it!"

"You don't buy what?" I asked him.

"I don't buy the whole deal," he snapped.

"*What* whole deal?" I asked.

"Christianity," he said. "Why are all these people here in the name of Christianity?"

There this guy stood in his $350 suit, probably having put $2 in the offering plate, a guy who was known for looking at every woman in the world except his wife, a guy who drove a $35,000 Mercedes and lived in a half-million-dollar house, and he was telling me he didn't buy it!

"Do you think the people here have a lot of needs?" I asked.

"Do they ever!" he said.

"That," I said, "is why they are here—because they have needs. Do *you* have needs?"

"Well . . . " he stammered.

"That," I said, "is why *you* ought to be here as well."

If you ever found a perfect church, somebody would come along and join it and mess it up. That's because Christians aren't perfect—they're in process.

NOT SEPARATISTS; THE SAME

Another distortion of Christianity is practiced by the pharisaical separatists. The Pharisees were separatists. They stayed away from anything and everything that even smelled of being "unclean." If there was a bar down the street, they would cross to the other side to keep from being contaminated by it. They avoided all contact with anyone who wasn't as "pure" as they were, and they wouldn't associate with or be seen with anyone who didn't believe exactly as they did. They did manage to keep "clean," but not without being "weird."

Paul wrote to the Thessalonians, "Abstain from every form of evil" (1 Thes. 5:22). Unfortunately, that is often translated, "appearance of evil." There is no way anyone can stay away from every "appearance of evil." The proper translation is *form*. Stay away from every *form* of evil —from evil forms, from evil practices, from practicing evil.

The *appearance* of evil could be anything. If you left your car sitting in front of your house on Sunday morning, it could be the appearance of evil. Even though you rode to church with a friend, people could say, "Oh, look, he didn't go to church today."

To use another example, I often stick a toothpick in my mouth, especially when I haven't eaten, because it makes me feel as if I have. A good friend of mine has a habit of puffing on his pen or pencil as if it's a cigarette, and I've picked it up. So someone might see me driving down the road, puffing away on my toothpick, but would that be an "appearance of evil"?

The separatism of the Pharisees must be replaced by the realization that we are the same as our fellow strugglers. We who are Christians have the same things going for us and the same things going against us as nonbelievers do. The *only* difference between us is that we have the hope that we're going to get through the problems of life, whereas the nonbeliever isn't sure.

So often I hear people say, "But you don't understand. I just don't have anything in common with nonbelievers anymore. When I became a Christian my nonbelieving friends and I drifted apart." In most cases the nonbelievers had nothing to do with the drifting. The believer friend got "weird" and began to separate himself. He began to walk, talk, and act differently, with that same old attitude the Pharisees had, as though he were different.

We are not different. We are just the same. We have house payments; they have house payments. We have mates; they have mates. We have bills; they have bills. We've got problems; they've got problems.

Something else I hear is, "We shouldn't share our problems with nonbelievers, because then they'll think Christianity doesn't work." How does Christianity work if not in the midst of problems? To say that Christianity is working when everything is going smoothly is a distortion. People usually come to the Lord when things get rough, and Christianity is best demonstrated when life is the toughest. We are all the same—we all have a pulse—and we can talk with the nonbeliever about his problems *and* our problems.

Some people take on a rather pompous attitude, even among other believers. "You couldn't possibly understand," they say. "If only you had been a believer as long as I have, and had gone down as deep and stayed down as long as I have, then you would understand." Christianity is not a complex deal. A lot of ministers would like you to believe it is, as they tell you they wish they had time to *really* get into some issue, but basically it's very simple. Christianity is people gathered together, trying to figure out how to come into a relationship with God, and once they have, trying to get their act together. It's God loving people and saying, "I want a relationship with you." It's people rebelling against God and then finally saying, "Nothing else works; I accept Your offer."

It's simple, so simple it's almost scary. "But I am afraid," Paul writes, "lest as the serpent deceived Eve by his craftiness, your minds would be led astray from the simplicity and purity of devotion to Christ" (2 Cor. 11:3). Satan wants us to think Christianity is complex. God wants us to know it's not.

NOT PUSHERS; SHARERS

The final distortion is that Christians are a bunch of "pushers"—that we push people into believing and accepting what the Bible says. We are not pushers—we are sharers. We are trying to draw people to the truth, not convert them and get them on the next bus to heaven.

"I have to ask you a question," a non-Christian friend of mine said to me. "How do you know the Bible is true? Everyone keeps telling me things are true because the Bible says they are true, but how do I know the *Bible's* true?"

I told him five reasons why I believe the Bible is the Word of God and therefore true. He replied, "No one's ever told me anything like that in my life, and I've been around Christians for the last twelve years. They just keep telling me I need to do this and I need to do that and pushing me to do it."

"I know what you mean," I said. "Christians can be pretty pushy creatures." But God doesn't want us to push. All He wants us to do is share the truth with people, live it out in our lifestyles, and then sit back and watch things happen.

DISTORTION OR DISTINCTION

The distortion is this: "Christianity is a ritual with regulations." The distinctive is this: "Christianity is a Person with principles of life that work." Our job as Christians is to turn the distortion of ritual and regulation into the distinction of the Person of Christ with biblical principles that work.

Agree with people when they get upset with religiosity; say, "You're right, I don't like that either." Then share with them what Christianity is really all about. Jesus wasn't big on religiosity either. He didn't walk around with a faraway look in His eye, saying, "Yes, beloved," as He is often portrayed on television. He was a real, live Person, and He did real-life things.

Radical Christianity is a relationship with the God-Man Jesus Christ. Turn the ritual into a Person, and turn the regulations—the system of do's and don'ts—into principles of life that work.

Whatever principles are in the Bible are there for our own good—for God's glory and our good. That's incredible. If you choose to be wise and follow the principles, you'll win. If you choose to be foolish and ignore the principles, you'll lose. It's that simple.

Anything other than that is a distortion, and we must do everything we can to turn the distortion into a distinctive. To do that we need to hunger and thirst for righteousness. Christ said, "Blessed are those who hunger and thirst for righteousness, for they shall be satisfied" (Matt. 5:6). Blessed are those who hunger and thirst for Christ, the only truly righteous Person, and for Christlikeness, which comes from following the principles of life by which He lived. Those people shall be satisfied.

A lady shared an amazing testimony with me not long ago. For several weeks she had been suffering a bout with a recurring disease. "You know, " she said, "I'm not sure if I'm losing my faith or gaining it, because my attitude this time is so different from what it was when I suffered with this in the past." I knew she and her family had all come into a relationship with the Lord over the last year and a half, and I could hardly contain myself. "My problem is," she continued, "that when this used to hit me, I would work as hard as I could because I wanted to get through it. Now I still want to get better, but if I don't, it's all right. Is that bad?"

"No," I said. "That's great! You are experiencing the peace of God that can only come from distinctive Christianity—a relationship with the Person of Christ and principles of life that make it work." When I see or hear about people like that, who come into a relationship with Christ and make life work, even in a crisis, I'm encouraged. I'm encouraged to stick around a little longer, and study a little harder, and speak a little more—because radical Christianity works.

Have you come into a relationship with Christ? Is your life working? Remember that real Christianity is having a relationship with a Person and following biblical principles of life that work.

In other words, it's radical.

APPENDIX
LIVING THE RADICAL CHRISTIAN LIFE:
THE 100% GOD, 100% MAN CONCEPT

There are two extremes in Christianity. Those at one end say that God does it all—that God lives the radical Christian lifestyle *for* us. The other side says that man does it all, that man lives the radical Christian lifestyle for himself. Between those two extremes is an enormous gap. In order to grow as Christians, to become increasingly Christ-centered, to live the radical Christian life, we must learn to live in that gap and to balance the two extremes.

There are extremes in almost every area of Christianity. On the question of women and their role in the church, one side says women should do everything, including serving as deacons, elders, or pastors; the other side says women shouldn't do anything except make coffee and teach children in Sunday School. On speaking in tongues, one side says you *must* in order to experience the fullness of God; the other says we must cut out the tongue of anyone who speaks in tongues. In the area of evangelism, one side won't share its faith even when the door is wide open with a "Welcome" sign on it; the other side picks the lock and breaks the door down, even when it has a "Do Not Enter" sign on it.

Where demonology is concerned, those at one extreme

think demons are simply a figure of speech and the devil is just a force. Their attitude toward both is, "Ignore them and they'll go away." Those at the other extreme think the devil and his demons are everywhere. Their approach is, "When in doubt, cast it out!"

When it comes to the Bible, those at one extreme say the *King James Version* is the only authentic one, and that if you're reading some other version, you aren't really reading the Bible. At the other extreme any version, even any *per*version, is fine; you can even write your own. There is another gap in the church between those who think the church should be a small, tightly knit group, and those who believe small groups aren't needed at all. The latter side says there is no need to equip or encourage people during the week; just have a great big celebration on Sunday and pump them up.

All of these gaps are spinoffs from the pinnacle of extremes: Who lives the Christian life—God or man? Where does God's work end and my work begin? Where does my work end and God's work begin? Who does what, and when?

The miracle of Lazarus' resurrection gives us a beautiful example of who does what, and when. When Jesus met Lazarus' sisters, Mary and Martha, and the others who were mourning Lazarus' death, He asked them, "Where have you laid him?" (John 11:34)

"Lord, come and see," they replied (v. 34). Jesus knew where Lazarus was—He had made the cave where they had buried Lazarus. But He wanted people to get involved in the process.

When the group arrived at the tomb, Jesus said, "Remove the stone" (v. 39). Certainly He could have taken care of the stone too, but again He wanted people to be involved. Once the tomb was open Jesus said, "Lazarus, come forth" (v. 43), and out walked Lazarus, bound hand and foot with grave-cloths. "Unbind him, and let him go," Jesus instructed them (v. 44).

Notice who does what here. Jesus had the crowd do

everything they could do, and He did everything they couldn't do. He didn't have the crowd tell Lazarus to get up. He did what only the God-Man could. But He did have them tell Him where the tomb was, remove the stone, and unbind the risen Lazarus. He had people do all things that were possible for them to do, and God did the impossible.

So man does it all, *and* God does it all. God and man work together. God does 100%, and man does 100%. God's 100% is a whole lot more than man's, but it's still a 100%-100% deal.

I grew up at the "man does it all" extreme, with a long list of do's and don'ts. When I realized that that wasn't right, that I didn't have to do it all, I shifted to the other extreme. That's the nature of extremes—we swing like pendulums from one side to the other. When I swung over, I "gave everything" to God. I totally "surrendered."

"God," I prayed, "If You don't do it, it won't get done." And it *didn't* get done.

THE WOERS AND THE WOWERS

Christians on the "man does it all" side often act like Pharisees. Their greatest concern is who's right and who's wrong, and they always have a scorecard and pencil in hand. On the "God does it all" side are the mystics, who sit around waiting to experience the Lord and wondering whether they have *really* believed.

On the "man does it" side, God is a tyrant who stalks around with His angelic gestapo, ready to nail you if you blow it. On the other side He is a genie, and all you have to do is make a wish and claim it and it's yours.

On the "man does it" side, perfection is attained by following a code of conduct. At the other extreme perfection comes through an experience. Both sides are trying for what they believe is first-class citizenship in heaven, and they think anyone who hasn't done what they've done or felt what they've felt is second class. Other Christians are constantly intimidated by people who live at these perfection extremes, and are therefore unable to grow. Often they become disgusted and discard Christianity completely.

This was true of a woman I counseled several years ago. She was falling apart. She'd had it, and as far as she was concerned there was no reason to go on with Christianity. She was frustrated, furious with the whole deal. "I just can't live the Christian life," she said.

"Why can't you?" I asked.

"Because I can't keep up with what's right and what's wrong," she replied.

"And what rights and wrongs can't you keep up with?" I asked. She then named all kinds of things that are not even mentioned in the Bible. Someone had imposed a list of do's and don'ts on her that had nothing to do with Christianity. She was a victim of the "man does it all" extreme.

One day as I was leaving to go to lunch, I received an emergency phone call. A prominent man in the area had just shot, but fortunately not killed, his wife. After the shooting he was in a catatonic state and hadn't spoken at all except to say that he wanted to talk to me.

I left immediately and went over to talk to him. I discovered that the church he was involved in had taught him to "Let go and let God." They told him that if he gave everything to God, God would control it and cause it to prosper. He would be the best, and his business would multiply. He had believed them, had hocked everything he owned, and had sat back and waited for God to do it all. When God didn't do it all, the man went sideways and started shooting everything in sight—including his wife. He was a victim of the "God does it all" extreme.

I call these two extremes the "Woers" and the "Wowers." The Woers are those on the "man does it all" extreme. They try to do it all, and when they fail they cry out, "Woe is me, for I am undone." The Wowers are those on the "God does ıt all" extreme. They leave everything to God and always seem excited. "Wow, I'm doing great," they exclaim.

Neither the Woers nor the Wowers are living in reality. Both are missing the balance of Scripture. Paul was aware of these extremes as he wrote to the New Testament churches, and he fought hard to eliminate them and fill in the gap. In the Book of Galatians he lays out the "man does it all" extreme, in Colossians he examines the "God does it all" extreme, and in Ephesians and Romans he balances them out and tells us how to live in between.

THE BALANCE

Therefore let no one act as your judge in regard to food or drink or in respect to a festival or a new moon or a Sabbath Day—things which are a mere shadow of what is to come: but the substance belongs to Christ. Let no one keep defrauding you of your prize by delighting themselves in self-abasement and the worship of the angels, taking his stand on visions he has seen, inflated without cause by his fleshly mind, and not holding fast to the head, from whom the entire body, being supplied and held together by the joints and ligaments, grows with a growth which is from God (Col. 2:16-19).

The rules and regulations of man are the "mere shadow" of what is to come. Now that Christ has come, Paul says, we don't need to be caught up in shadowy things. We aren't to let anyone intimidate us concerning our "prize," the joy and excitement and eternal life we have because of Christ. The Woers try to steal our prize by "delighting themselves in self-abasement," while the Wowers do so by "the worship of angels" and "visions." In order to have balance we must reject both and jump into the middle, into Christ, between "God does it all" and "man does it all."

THE PRESENT OF GOD

A balanced picture of God's work and man's work is seen in the first chapter of 2 Peter. Peter begins by looking at God's work, at the gift He has given to every believer: "Seeing that His divine power has granted to us everything pertaining to life and godliness, through the true knowledge of Him who called us by His own glory and excellence" (2 Peter 1:3). Think about that for a minute. God has given us each a present, the present of His divine power, and that power provides everything we need to live the Christian life. If we have accepted Jesus Christ as our personal Saviour, we have all that is necessary for life and godliness. There is no missing piece, no book, class, seminar, or speaker that can add to the picture or give us anything more. We have it all.

"For by these [His glory and excellence] He had granted to us His precious and magnificent promises, in order that by them [His promises] you might become partakers of the divine nature, having escaped the corruption that is in the world by lust" (2 Peter 1:4, brackets added). God's power enables us to obtain the divine nature, to actually take hold of, participate in, and share God's character. No matter what our circumstances are, our character can reflect His. We have God's power to live the radical Christian life and to reflect Him as we do so, even in the midst of corruption.

THE PRACTICE OF MAN

Having looked at God's work, Peter goes on to present man's work when he writes, "Now for this very reason also, applying all diligence, in your faith supply . . ." (2 Peter 1:5). He goes on to list the qualities man is, with all diligence, to supply to his faith—the things he is to practice.

The word for *supply* means to totally sponsor, to pick up the final bill for something. It was used in the Greek when someone sponsored a play or a musical event. The head of state would go to a Roman citizen and say, "We are putting on a big production in September, and so you can prove your outstanding citizenship, we would like you to underwrite it." The head of state knew whom to ask, and those he asked made lavish provisions to prove what exemplary citizens they were.

Peter says we are to *supply,* to totally sponsor, the following things: "Moral excellence [virtue], and in your moral excellence, knowledge; and in your knowledge, self-control, and in your self-control, perseverance, and in your perseverance, godliness; and in your godliness, brotherly kindness, and in your brotherly kindness, Christian love" (2 Peter 1:5-7). God has given us the power to supply all those things to our faith, and now He wants us to underwrite them, to lavishly provide them.

Moral excellence, or virtue, carries here the idea of self-declaration. It's declaring yourself to be on God's team. Once you have accepted Christ and come into a relationship with God, you can declare, "I have committed my life to Jesus Christ." The *knowledge* Peter lists next is practical knowledge, knowledge about life. It is supplied by learning truth, by listening, reading, and studying it. *Self-control* means "self-strength." It's not a sinful, selfish strength, but the resource God gives so that you can control yourself.

Perseverance is "hanging in there," not letting go. *Godliness* is acting out what you know. The Christian life must be lived in relationship, not in a vacuum, so supply *brotherly kindness.* Finally, in your brotherly kindness, supply *Christian love*— God's love.

The present of God to you is the power to live the Christian life. The practice you are to perform is to diligently add the above qualities to your faith. It's 100% God, His present—and 100% man, your practice.

Peter then lists the results of supplying these things to our faith:

For if these qualities are yours and are increasing, they render you neither useless nor unfruitful in the true knowledge of our Lord Jesus Christ. For he who lacks these qualities is blind [he can't see where he is] or short-sighted [he can't see where he is going], having forgotten his purification from his former sins [he can't see where he has been]. Therefore, brethren, be all the more diligent to make certain about His calling and choosing you [make certain you have received His present]; for as long as you practice these things, you will never stumble; for in this way the entrance into the eternal kingdom of our Lord and Saviour Jesus Christ will be abundantly supplied to you (2 Peter 1:8-11, brackets added).

Peter uses the word *supply* again, but this time God is doing the supplying. We are to supply certain things to our faith, and then God supplies a special entrance for us into His kingdom.

When a victorious athlete returned home from the early Olympic games, his city would cut a hole in its wall through which he could enter. It was his opening, his special entrance, and no one else was allowed to use it. Peter is saying the same thing. If we take God's present and His power and then practice the qualities we are to supply to our faith, God will make a "hole" in the wall of His kingdom for us. It will be our special entrance; no one else will be allowed to use it, and when we walk through it there will be a heavenly shout.

Growth in the Christian life requires only two things—a present from God and practice from us. It's so simple that we stumble all over ourselves and it slips by. We're too busy trying to do things perfectly. "Oh," we moan, "if I could just figure out what God's will is"—and we forget the fact that He's already given it to us. We're too busy waiting around for God to make a move, asking, "Do something, God. Please, anything. Just a clue, like a little lightning." We live in the extremes, not in the gap between the extremes where God does His part and we do ours.

LIVING IN THE GAP: GOD'S 100%

To grow as Christians, we must first ask ourselves, "Have I received God's present?"

If I were to offer you a $100 bill as a gift, it would not actually be yours until you took it out of my hand. I could hold it out to you and wave it around, but until you reached out and received it, it wouldn't be yours. Similarly, God offers you the gift of Jesus Christ as your personal payment for sin; but you must accept His payment. God wants to come into your life and pay for all the garbage and all the guilt. All He wants you to do is admit that you need Him, that you need His Son, and accept His payment.

The second question on the "100% God" side is, "Are you counting on it?" You could carry a $100 bill around in your pocket forever, but it wouldn't do you any good if you never used it. When you receive the present of God, you have the power to live the Christian life, but in order for it to do you any good you have to use it. You need to think about it, talk about it, sing about it, shout about it. Take it into account as you make decisions. God wants you to use His power to carry out His purposes for your life.

You are an unrepeatable miracle of God. There is no one else like you, and there will never be anyone else like you. God has a unique message to bring to the world that only you can deliver. So count on His present, His power, and His purpose for you.

MAN'S 100%

On the "100% man" side is what *you* do. The Bible says everything you do is to be done to the glory of God in order to reflect Him to the world. Glory involves an opinion or estimation, and everything you do is an opinion or estimation of what God is all about. If you operate in the extremes, you're broadcasting the opinion that God works that way, with the result that people are turned off and driven away from Him. If you live in the gap and hang onto the balance, people are turned on and drawn toward Him.

The Scripture is filled with countless examples of living in the gap and maintaining the balance. "By faith Noah, being warned by God about things not yet seen, in reverence prepared an ark for the salvation of his household, by which he condemned the world, and became an heir of the righteousness which is according to faith" (Heb. 11:7). If Noah had not been willing to build the ark, having faith that God was going to bring the water and make the ark float on top of it, he and his family would have gone under with the rest of the world. I can just hear Noah's neighbors harassing him: "Noah, what are you doing? You're building a boat? What's a boat? There's going to be a flood? What's a flood? A lot of water coming out of the sky? Right, Noah. Have you seen your shrink lately?"

Maybe a few actually encouraged him. "Boy, Noah, whatever you're into, it's fine with me. If you want to build a boat to float on water that's going to fall from heaven, that's great. You're doing a good job."

I can't imagine Noah responding with, "Oh, no, I didn't do it. God did it. God built the boat. I was just here praying, and God came and put this thing together." I *can* imagine him saying, "Thanks. This has been a grueling job. I've gotten splinters, smashed my thumb a couple of times, and a few days ago I lost my balance and fell off the ladder. But it *is* looking good, isn't it? I built it by faith that God is going to use it." That's the 100% God, 100% man concept.

"Work out your salvation with fear and trembling" (Phil. 2:12). To work out your salvation means to live out that which is inside you. Work it out in your life. Fortunately that passage goes on, "For it is God who is at work in you, both to will and to work for His good pleasure" (Phil. 2:13). God is also working it out in your life. That's the 100% God, 100% man concept too.

In the first three chapters of Ephesians, Paul lists the

things God has done for us: He has blessed us with every spiritual blessing, chosen us, adopted us as sons, bestowed His grace on us, seated us in the heavenly places, and given us access to His very throne. In all three chapters there is not one thing we are to do, only what God has done for us. Then, in the last three chapters, there are thirty-three things we are to do! First Paul says, "Look at the presents God has given you, the power He has given you to live the Christian life." Then he says, "Now act like it!" That is also the 100% God, 100% man concept.

"Therefore, laying aside falsehood, speak truth, each one of you, with his neighbor, for we are members of one another. . . . Let him who steals steal no longer; but rather let him labor, performing with his own hands what is good, in order that he may have something to share with him who has need" (Eph. 4:25, 28). Paul says to put off and put on. Don't sit around and wait for God to zap you, and don't go out and try to "gut it out" on your own. By the power of God, put off the old and put on the new. If you're lying, stop lying and start telling the truth. If you're stealing, stop stealing and start working. Again it's the 100% God, 100% man concept.

LEARNING OUR LESSON

The concept is simple, and it's reiterated time and again in Scripture. But most of us come to understand it only after we have crashed and burned in one of the extremes and are staggering around in the wreckage. We need to learn a lesson from some four-footed friends.

A lion, a fox, and a hyena were moving through the jungle, collecting their dinner. When they were done they made a big pile of all the animals they had killed, then sat back to relax. A few minutes later the lion said, "Mr. Hyena, why don't you go over and divide our pile into three equal parts?"

"Sure," said the hyena, who was getting hungry. He quickly separated the dead animals into three equal piles.

Immediately the lion sprang to his feet, pounced on the hyena, and killed him.

The lion then put the three piles back together, threw the hyena on top, and said to the fox, "Mr. Fox, why don't you go over and divide our pile into two equal parts?" The fox didn't say anything. He just moved over to the pile and shuffled through the dead animals until he had two piles. In his pile he had one dead crow, and in the lion's pile was everything else.

The lion smiled. "Mr. Fox," he said, "how did you learn to divide so equally?"

"The hyena taught me," answered the fox.

I have a question for you. How many hyenas does it take before you learn? How much wreckage and destruction and heartache does it take before you wake up and start living in the gap?

There are two extremes. One is that God does it all. The other is that man does it all. In order to grow as Christians and to have a radical Christian lifestyle, we must live in balance—accepting God's present and including our practice. That's the 100% God, 100% man concept.